Books by Sharon Kizziah-Holmes

RIDE THE STORM

Published by Writers Club Press

A STAR
THAT TWINKLED
BUT NEVER GOT TO SHINE

By Sharon Kizziah-Holmes

A&S Publishing

Published by A & S Publishing
1352 E. Sunshine
Springfield, MO 65804
tommykizziah.com

ISBN 0-9769528-0-7

First A & S Trade Paperback Printing: July 2005

Printed in the United States of America

Cover Art by Sharon Kizziah-Holmes
Special acknowledgement to Judy Miller
Perfection Printing & Design
Springfield, MO

With all of my gratitude, admiration and love, I dedicate this book to my precious mother Frances P. Kizziah

Thank you for life, Mommy.

Acknowledgments

My Thanks:

To the West Coast Ramblers. Dad's best years in the music business were with you. You stood by his side and were there when he needed you.

Buddy and Opal Simmons, your input on this book is priceless. I will always be grateful for time you took to put things together for me and for staying lifetime friends with my folks and me. I love you both and Don and Larry.

Evelyn Kinnee, you sent me your treasured seventy-eight records of the West Coast Ramblers and Dad. You'll never know how much that means to me.

Skipper Montee, you shared stories with me about your years with the West Coast Ramblers. I love every one of them. I'm glad we got in touch after all these years.

Many thanks to my husband Dennis for standing beside me in life and encouraging me to finish this four year project. You are my love.

To Ozarks Romance Authors for helping me hone my writing, I couldn't have learned without you.

Norma, you're the best friend a girl can have. You are an angel. Thank you for your support and love.

To my copy, grammar and everything else editor Connie Foster, you made it better and I appreciate you.

My brother's Johnny and Benny. I love you and thanks for having faith in your little sister.

A Note From The Author

Hi,

I hope you enjoy the book, pictures and CD. It took me a few years to get it all together, but sharing Dad's story and music with others makes it all worth the time.

Some folks have questioned me about how much of the book is actually true. I have to say, most of it. The events all really happened. Births, deaths, weddings, babies, travels, shows, people, (though some of their names may have been changed) family events... all real. Of course, the dates and times may not be right on the dot, and to write it in story form I had to make up the conversations, but the general story is the way it truly was.

My mother, brothers, aunts, uncles, members of WCR and lots of friends and other family members were my sources for information. I appreciate them all so much for helping me.

Thank you for taking the time to learn about my Dad, Mom and our family. Take time to visit our website at www.tommykizziah.com

Sincerely,
Sharon Kizziah-Holmes

CHAPTER 1

Summer 1953

Tommy Kizziah felt perspiration gather between his shoulder blades under the leather strap of his Gibson 335. From the bandstand he glanced out at the crowd of over two thousand fans.

Sounds of electric guitars being tuned, a fiddle bow drawn across its strings and the tam... tam... tam of the drummer warming up, echoed through the building. He waited for the radio engineer's signal to tell him when it was time to start the show.

The man held up three fingers. Tommy turned his attention to the musicians who were making their last minute adjustments. "Here we go, boys." Two fingers popped up, one, then the man pointed at the band and nodded.

The lively tone of Evelyn's steel guitar kicked off the group's theme song, *Long Tom Boogie*. Tommy smiled and stepped up to the microphone. His deep voice carried over the loud speakers to his live audience, and through radio speakers in the living rooms of thousands of folks listening at home. "A great big Saturday night howdy to ya', neighbors!"

An explosion of applause cracked the smoky, dim atmosphere of the hall. People of all shapes and sizes made their way to the giant hardwood dance floor.

"Welcome to Wagon Wheel Park, where we're coming to you live over KGW. I'm Tommy Kizziah with the West Coast Ramblers, and tonight our special guest is Willie Nelson."

* * *

December 5, 1915

Rebeka Jane Hickey remembered the day she married Elick Alonzo Kizziah in 1903. Their small, dirt floored, four-room house, they still lived in, rested on the Tennessee river. It was the second dwelling on the road leading to Rockwood, TN from Jackson Landing in Roane County.

Janie, as everyone called her, was pleased her family lived so close to the first dwelling. Lon's mother, Lydia, and his three younger brothers occupied it. Why, you could almost throw a rock and hit Lyd's house.

She and Lon had four sons that she loved with all her heart. Isaac Enoch (called Ike), William Franklin (Bill), Jack Wilder (Jack), and Major John (Red). Two babies, born before Ike, died infant deaths. She'd been heartbroken when she lost the little things.

This day will be different, she thought, as she lay on the bed in her home, gazing up at her husband. His smile went from ear to ear as he held the tiny newborn in his arms.

"It's another boy, Janie. What do you want to name him?"

Lon didn't know, but she already knew what she would call him. If it had been a girl, she would have named her Mary Lydia after her mother-in-law, but it was a boy.

"Thomas Henry," she whispered when Lon placed the bundle in her arms. "Thomas Henry Kizziah."

* * *

Sixteen months after Tommy arrived, Janie finally got the little girl she'd always wanted. Mary Lydia was born April 14, 1917. Life was complete.

One evening while Tommy toddled around, Janie carried Mary on her hip and listened to the music her family was making in the other room.

Lon played a lot of instruments, but that night he played the guitar. Jack, who was learning quickly, screeched out the tune on the fiddle and Bill, at eleven years old, plunked the banjo with skill.

She walked over to the old wood stove and checked the biscuits, browned to perfection. She put Mary down, got a dishtowel from the counter top and moved the hot morsels to the table. Beans and biscuits didn't make the best meal in the world, but it would fill their bellies.

Stifling the cough that threatened to wrack her lungs, she hollered over the music, "Okay, supper's ready!"

The family filtered into the small room, taking their seats one at a time. Janie gazed at the scruffy brood. She loved each and every one of them. She only wished she felt better so she could join in more of the fun.

Oh, she could still play the organ, but singing had been too hard the last few weeks. Every time she tried to take a deep breath, she'd cough.

Taking her seat, she looked at her husband. "Lon, I think I should go into town and see the doctor. I can't seem to shake this cold. Maybe he has some medicine he can give me. Do you think we can afford it?"

Lon dipped his biscuit into his beans and took a bite. "We'll make do. I'll take ya' in to see the doc tomorrow, Maw can watch the young'uns."

"Why don't y'all take Tommy in with ya. See if ol' doc can do anything for that cocked eye of his," Bill chided, then laughed and gave his brother a sideways glance.

Janie found herself always defending her youngest boy. "Now you leave that baby alone. He ain't even two years yet. Maybe his eye will fix itself."

"Momma, you know that ain't gonna happen," Ike said.

"Well, it might if we pray hard enough about it."

"I think he's retarded. Why, he cain't even talk right yet. You better pray about that, too, Maw."

She whacked Jack on the back of the head. "You boys stop it right now. You'd better be the ones prayin'. Prayin' for forgiveness. Talkin' about your brother like that. One of these days he'll be big enough to take care of himself. I bet you don't talk bad about him then."

The cough couldn't be stopped this time. She covered her mouth with her hand. It burned deep in her lungs when she finally caught her breath.

"Yep, we'll head out for town first thing in the mornin'," Lon announced.

* * *

"Well, what do ya' think, Doc?"

"She's got pneumonia, Lon. I'm going to give her some medicine that will make her some better. Actually, I feel like she's been through the worst of it already. You have one tough woman there."

Janie joined her husband and the doctor in the small office opposite the even smaller examination room. "Did I hear you say pneumonia?"

Lon put his arm around her shoulders. "Yep, but he's givin' you some medicine to help ya."

"You need to rest, Janie," the doctor warned, peering at her over his wire-framed spectacles. "I know you've got those babies, but the bigger boys can help you watch them. Lyd, too." He glanced at Lon. "You'll make sure she gets some rest, won't you?"

"Yes, sir, I'm sure Maw will watch the babies. I'm gonna leave in a couple of weeks. It's time for the medicine show to come through, and you know I play and sing on it every year. This year I'm takin' Bill and Jack with me."

"I think she'll be okay by that time. Just a few days rest is all she needs. Like I said, she's already over the worst of it."

Lon pulled a few dollars out of his pocket. "How much do we owe ya, Doc?"

The old man scratched his head. "I know you're working at the Strickland farm, but are you still doing carpentry work on the side?"

"Sure 'nuff."

"Did you see that the roof on my porch out front is trying to fall down?"

"I noticed it."

"How about you fix that for me, and we'll call it even."

A smile crossed Lon's lips. "That sounds good. The boys and me'll be here Saturday mornin'. It'll only take a few hours."

The doctor offered a handshake. "Good enough."

Janie followed her husband to their old battered pickup. She climbed onto the dusty seat then shut the door. "I'm feelin' better already. Just knowin' the worst is over eases my mind."

"Doc was right, you know. You are a tough gal. You've been sicker than a dog, and didn't stop doin' what you needed to do. I love ya', Janie."

A grin lifted the corners of her mouth. She knew Lon appreciated her. "I love you, too."

* * *

When the medicine show wagon pulled in front of the house, Janie's heart sank. It was time for most of her family to leave for the summer. She felt a tug at her skirt as Red stood shyly behind her. Tommy, being the inquisitive two-year-old, climbed up the wagon steps before she could catch him. "Jack, get T.H. would you?"

"Sure, Maw." Jack took his youngest brother by the arm. "Come on, Tom. You cain't go with us. This trip is only for big boys."

Janie imagined Jack did feel pretty grown up because he was getting to go on his first show. For an eight-year-old boy, he was a responsible child, and wanted to make his daddy proud. Her too, of course, but his daddy was his idol.

Lon placed the last of the supplies into the wagon. Taking long strides, his tall frame came closer to her. He was such a handsome man, and her boys would be too.

"It's time to go, Janie. You let Maw help ya with the little ones. I'll send ya money when I can. The more tonic we sell, the more we make, and I'm hopin' that havin' the boys with me will inspire folks to buy."

"How long do you think you'll be gone? You know this is the first time I've ever been away from Jack and Bill."

He put his arms around her and pulled her close. "We'll be back in a few weeks." Humor shone in his eyes. "The boys'll be fine and so will you. Ike will be here to be the man of the house while I'm gone, and I'm sure the garden and the babies will keep you busy. The time'll fly by. I'll write ya."

For some reason, she didn't feel comforted, but she knew he was right. Time seemed to go by faster the older she got, and getting the garden started was going to be quite the chore.

Mr. Trench's voice rang through the air. "Let's go fella's, we got one more stop to make before we get out'o town."

Janie looked into her husband's deep brown eyes and accepted his good-by kiss. "I love ya, Lon."

He smiled and nodded. "Same cow hooked me."

Jack was already waiting on the wagon, eager to make his first trip. "Come on, Paw."

Lon climbed onto the wagon, and it pulled away with half her family resting on its creaky frame.

* * *

Tommy and Red were in the corner with the musical instruments Lon didn't take with him on the medicine show. For some reason Tom was fascinated with the old guitar. Janie figured it would do no harm for him to play with it. Even though two strings were broken, the four left could cause quite a racket when he plunked them.

Red didn't have much interest in making music, but he loved to watch his little brother pretend to perform. So he sat quietly on the dirt floor and listened while, not quite on key but loud and clear, his brother's sweet voice rang through the small dwelling.

"Jus a walk wif thee." Plunk, plunk, plunk, Jesus e my pwea"

It was her favorite hymn and she was pleased he knew at least that many words. "T.H. you're getting better all the time." Hopefully, Lon would take the time to teach Tom the same way he did Jack and Bill.

Lon loved their youngest boy, but it pained her that he thought the child wasn't as smart as the other boys. Everyone had thought Tom was retarded because he looked different, with his eye cocked up in his head, but he was smart.

A grin touched the corners of her mouth. Why, he wasn't even three yet and he was trying to teach himself how to play the guitar.

* * *

Janie bustled around trying to get the big meal ready. Today, her family would be together again. It was hard to believe summer had come and gone. Lon was right when he said the time would pass fast.

Mary was walking and trying to say momma. Tommy was talking good, but she was still concerned about his eye. She had hoped it would get better as he grew. Now she knew it wouldn't. Maybe when he got older they could afford to take him to a doctor that knew a little bit about eyes. She supposed he needed spectacles.

Tommy jumped up and down on the rickety old porch. "Maw, Maw, here they come."

Red's and Tom's little feet scampered away to meet the gang. She wiped her hands on her apron, picked up Mary, then crossed the short distance to the door. Her daughter on her hip, she stepped onto the porch and watched the wagon pull to a stop. Ike strolled out, said his hellos and helped unload.

Her heart beat wildly as it always did, when her husband

returned home from a trip. Lon stepped down and oh, what a sight he was. "Hello, husband." He approached, she gazed into his eyes and when he reached her, she put the baby down and gave him a kiss. "I've missed you something terrible."

He smiled and put his arms around her waist, "I've missed you, too, wife. How ya feelin'?"

"Better, the cough ain't as bad, and I can breathe now. I'm fine, don't worry."

"Paw, Paw!"

Janie smiled when Tommy came toward them. Lon released his grip around her and lifted his young son in the air.

Twirling the boy, Lon said, "Tom, you got so big while we were gone."

"Me big enough play music, Paw?"

Lon put the boy down and grinned. "Well, we'll have to see about that. Right now, me and you're brothers want some of your maw's home cookin'. We're hungry enough to eat a bear!"

Tommy, in his worn out hand me down overalls, toddled behind his father. He glanced at his little sister as she swayed back and forth and hung onto the porch so she wouldn't fall. "Papa's eat bear, Mary!" he proclaimed.

* * *

"Well, this is the last plank," Lon said, then hammered the board in place. "It sure will be nice to have a wood floor this winter instead of that ol' cold dirt."

"I guess having Jack and Bill on the show with you the last two years really did help in sales. Maybe next year, Tom can go. He's getting pretty good at singing, you know."

Lon stood, then met his wife's gaze. "Janie, you know I cain't take that boy. Everyone'll make fun of him cause he's so ugly, and they'd think he's retarded. Besides, he cain't play nothin'."

"That boy is not ugly, he just has a bad eye. He can sing,

and the only reason he can't play is because you won't teach him. Before he was three he was trying to play all by himself. He'll be five his next birthday, and he's smart, Lon, he can learn."

"Hon, I'm not tryin' to be mean, but I don't have time to fool with Tom when I have to practice with Jack and Bill, work on the Strickland farm and do all my chores around here."

"I know you do a lot, but you're just embarrassed because of his eye. Maybe we should get him some eye glasses, or take him to a doctor somewhere and see if that's what he needs."

"Janie, it's true, I don't like it when folks stare at us because of Tom, but we cain't afford no glasses. Hell, we just barely paid for this floor."

She tried to hide her sorrow. He was right, they had enough money to last them through the winter, but that was only if he could work some, too. Ike brought in a little money from helping at the general store in town. She was proud of the sixteen year old. Even though he liked girls and had a few coming around, he always handed over his small paycheck to his daddy to help with things around the house.

"Okay, Lon, but you've got to promise me that when you have a little time, you'll help Tom learn how to play. That doesn't cost anything."

Lon took a deep breath then released it. "Okay, I'll try."

At least that was more than he'd agreed to before, and that's all she could ask for.

* * *

Spring 1921

The leaves on the trees unfolded in green splendor. Wild flowers bloomed in the fields and Janie struggled for each breath. Sometimes it was worse than others, and today the wheezing was the most terrible of all.

Last year she lived with the on and off again effort it took for her to breathe, but this year it was more than she could reckon with. That's why Lon was taking her into town to see Doc again. Maybe he'd have the outcome of the tests he'd done.

Lon was supposed to leave for the medicine show again in a few weeks, but she didn't think she could make it without him unless she got some relief from the pressure in her chest.

"Come on, Hon, let's go," Lon urged.

Janie glanced at her mother-in-law. "Thanks for watching T.H. and Mary, Lyd I don't know what I'd do without you."

Lydia Kizziah reached out and patted Janie's hand. "You don't worry 'bout them babies. You just worry 'bout gettin' better."

Closing the truck door, Janie took a labored breath and replied, "I'll be fine. We'll see you later today."

By the time they got to town, Janie was breathing better. When they reached the doctor's, it was like nothing had ever hindered her lungs at all. She just didn't understand.

They drove up in front of Doc's brand new office. It was the first time she'd seen it since they finished building it.

Inside, the rooms were bright. The walls were painted white and it looked so clean. Doc even had a nurse now, and his wife greeted the patients.

"Mornin', Janie. You feeling under the weather?"

"Actually, right now I'm doing good. It comes and goes. As always."

"Well, you two just have a seat. Doc will be with you shortly. He just has one more to see before you."

Janie sat next to her husband in one of the new chairs. The cushions were soft and velvety and felt good against her body. If only she could feel this well every day, she'd be fine.

The nurse appeared. "Mrs. Kizziah, are you ready?"

"Yes, ma'am." She followed the woman in the white uniform to a small room. Lon stayed in the waiting area.

The doctor's helper took a thermometer out of a vile of

alcohol, rinsed it off in a new sink with running water, looked at it, shook it then studied it again. "Are you running a fever, Mrs. Kizziah?"

"I don't think so," Janie replied.

"Well, we'll check it to make sure."

Janie opened her mouth. The glass object was cold under her tongue.

"Now, you don't run off. I'll be right back. The doctor will be in shortly to give you the answers you've been waiting for."

Run off? Was that woman crazy? Where would she go? Especially with that thing sticking out her mouth. She smiled at her own silly thoughts and soon the nurse was back. The doctor followed right behind.

The woman took the thermometer. "No fever, Sir," she said then left the room.

"That's a good sign, Janie." He smiled and took her hand. "I hear you're having a hard time breathing again. This has been going on since you had that pneumonia three years ago, hasn't it?"

"Yes."

"I think I know why. All of the tests indicate that you're asthmatic."

"What in the world is that?"

"It's a disorder in your respiratory system. Bronchial asthma affects your lungs and such. You're probably allergic to something in the air around here."

"How come it never happened before the pneumonia?"

"Well, maybe that made you more susceptible to some allergies. It's a disease that can come on folks later in life."

"What can we do about it, Doc?"

"I'm afraid you're not going to like what I recommend. I think I'm going to get Lon in here and talk to you both about this." He left the room.

What in the world could be so bad that he wanted to talk to her husband about it, too? Was she going to die from this or something? She swallowed the lump in her throat and was relieved to see Lon enter the room with the doctor. She reached for his hand and his warm grip was comforting.

"Have a seat, Lon," the doctor said.

"What's this all about, Doc?" Lon's deep voice sounded stressed.

"Lon, Janie's got asthma. That's a lung disease. She's probably got some allergies to something in this area."

"So what do we need to do?"

The doctor took a deep breath and met Lon's gaze. "I think you should move."

"Move?"

Surprise was clear in her husband's voice. Surely the doctor wasn't serious.

"That's right, move," the doctor repeated. "It's too wet here. There are too many things in the air that can make her sick. Asthma can be a killer and Janie really needs to live in a hot dry climate."

Lon frowned. "Like where, Doc?"

The man didn't ponder. "Texas, maybe?"

On the way home she tried to convince her husband that she would get over the sickness and they didn't have to move, but he wouldn't listen.

"Don't argue with me, Janie. If the doc says we need to move to Texas, then we'll go to Texas."

"Lon, that will mean we'll have to leave your mamma and your brothers. They're our family, too. I rely on Lyd so much."

"Hon, Maw will understand. You cain't rely on anyone if you're dead. Then our young'uns won't have a mamma. Now, I know some folks in Dickens county Texas. I've only been there once, but the air is dry and that's where we'll go."

"What about the medicine show?"

"They'll get someone to take my place, and I'm sure I can find a show to do in Dickens County."

"But, Lon,"

"No buts! We're goin' to Texas!"

CHAPTER 2

Summer 1921

Not many trees dotted the landscape, and hot wind blew through the open windows of the truck. The boys had piled blankets in the back to make themselves as comfortable as possible, and they took turns riding up front now and then.

Lon watched the road and wiped a trickle of salty sweat from his face. It was only a couple of hours after daybreak, but it was already hot.

Mary was asleep in the seat, her hair stuck to her little face, and Janie looked pale and tired. Thank God, they only had fifty more miles to go before they got to Dickens, Texas.

Lon prayed that moving to Texas was the right decision. Of course, as far as Janie's health went, it was right, but the money was another consideration. He bought a truck he thought would make the trip with no problems, and with gas and food, he was down to his last twenty-five dollars.

It was too late in the year to find a medicine show to go on, but he was in hopes that he could get some carpentry work. Ike could work, too, and that would help.

A knock on the back truck-cab window drew his attention. When he turned, he saw Bill's face. His faint voice forced itself through the glass.

"Paw, can we stop? Tom's gotta' pee. Me, too."

He hated to pull over, being as close as they were, but he had to admit he needed to stretch and Janie probably did, too.

He motioned for Bill to sit down, then pulled to the side of the road. The roadside did little to protect them from being seen while relieving themselves, but there wasn't another car for miles around.

It was quiet without the road noise and wind blowing around them. When he turned off the engine, the silence of the prairie surrounded them. The boy's quickly jumped out of the truck.

"You boys be careful of them rattlesnakes. There's plenty of 'em out here,' Lon warned, joining them.

Tom studied the ground. "I ain't never seen a rattler, Paw."

"Well, I'm sure you'll see one soon enough in this country, T. H."

"How much further is it to Dickens, Paw?" Red asked.

"Only another hour or so."

"Good," Ike said, "I'm tuckered. I just wanna lay down someplace and sleep."

"Let's get back in the truck and be on our way," Lon instructed, "The longer we stay here, the longer it'll take us to get there. Janie, you ready?" He approached his wife and daughter.

"I'm ready, Lon."

His stomach tightened with worry. She seemed so tired and weak. Doc said the trip might be hard on her. Maybe after a few days rest she'd be better. "You okay, Hon?"

"I'll be fine. I just lost my breakfast, that's all. Must be all this riding that's making my stomach do flip flops."

He opened the door for her and lifted Mary into the cab. "When we get there, I want you to go straight to bed. You hear me?" He made his way to the driver's side, started the truck and pulled onto the highway.

Janie brushed fine tendrils of hair off of Mary's face. "I don't know that I'll feel right going to bed this early in the day. In a stranger's house no less!"

"Now, Ossie McCoy said they had plenty of room for us.

They have an upstairs to their house and said we could stay up there 'till we find us a place. Don't you worry about nothin'. You just get well."

She inhaled a deep breath. "It sure is nice to be able to breathe. I noticed earlier this mornin' that the weight on my chest is lighter."

At that moment Lon decided that no matter what happened, if Janie would be well again, the decision to move was the right one.

* * *

Janie pulled the chain on the toilet. Pleased they found a house in only three weeks, and one with the luxury of an inside bathroom and electricity, something they'd never had before. The landlord promised to let Lon and the boys work off the rent until jobs could be found. The folks in Texas seemed real nice.

However, all of their kindness couldn't hide the fact that she'd just lost her breakfast again. She recognized the signs and had to break the news to Lon.

Rounding the corner, then entering the kitchen where the family was finishing their biscuits and gravy, she took her place at the table. "Lon?"

"Um-hmm."

"You know that crib we left behind. The one we didn't think we'd need again?"

"Yep," he answered, still unaware.

"Can you build another one?"

"Sure, who nee…"

The look on his face told her he understood. "That's one reason the trip was so hard on me. I'm going to have another baby."

Mary clapped her hands. "Baby! Baby! Mamma have baby!"

Lon put his last bite in his mouth, chewed then swallowed.

"Janie, I cain't say this is great news, but we'll just have to make the best of it. When do you think it'll come?"

"I'd say early spring. Maybe even February."

He glanced around the wooden kitchen table at their six children. "Guess I'll have to build a highchair, too," he claimed with a smile.

* * *

Spring 1922

Tommy was excited for the new baby to come. It was fun playing with Mary, but he hoped he'd get a little brother. He was tired of being the youngest boy and getting made fun of all the time. Why did his stupid ol' eyeball have to be funny, anyway?

All he wanted to do was play music like his brothers. His daddy didn't have time during the winter to teach him how to play the guitar, and soon the baby would come, then it would be time for them all to leave on the new medicine show. He was going on seven years old now, so he guessed he'd just have to learn by himself.

"Thomas Henry! What you thinkin' about, boy? I've been callin' you."

The deep voice startled him. "Sorry, Paw."

"Go tell Ike to fetch the midwife. You're mamma's gonna have the baby."

Tommy couldn't seem to move his feet. The baby was coming!

"Move, boy!"

With a little prod from his paw, he scurried through the house, out the front door, jumped off the porch and ran toward his oldest brother. "Ike, Ike!"

Ike was bent over under the hood of an old car he'd just bought. He rose up and wiped his hands on a cloth. "What is it, Tom?"

He fought to steady his breathing. "It-it's Maw! She's

havin' the baby. Paw said for you to go get the midwife."

Putting the hood down, Ike said, "I hope this old jalopy will make it over there and back."

"Take Paw's truck, Ike. Just hurry!"

"Tom, you need to calm down," Ike commented as he got into the car. "Maw's had plenty of babies. She'll be fine."

"Yeah, but I ain't never had a little brother before."

Ike smiled. "Odds are it's another girl, Tom," he said and started the engine. "I wouldn't get my hopes up if I were you."

Tommy's stomach filled with butterflies. What if it was a girl? Then he'd still be the runt boy. No, it was a boy. He just knew it. "Shut up, Ike. I'm havin' a little brother!" He turned and ran back to the house.

Tommy sat impatiently and waited for the baby to be born. What was taking so long? Whatever it was, it didn't seem to bother Bill and Jack. They were making music like nothing else was going on. Red was playing a silly game with Mary, and Ike was off with some girl.

Tom looked up. What was that noise? He scooted closer to the edge of the couch and listened. Was it? It was! "Hey, the baby's cryin'. Listen, he's here!"

Silence filled the living room when Bill and Jack put down their instruments. Sure enough, Tom heard the baby's cry again. "See, I told ya," he boasted to his siblings and hopped off the couch. "I'm gonna go see if it's a boy!"

Jack put his hand on Tom's shoulder. "You'd better stay outta' there till they're done. Paw'll have your hide."

At that moment, Tommy heard the bedroom door open and out stepped his paw with a bundle of blankets in his arms.

"Is that the baby, Paw?"

"Sure is, Tom."

"What is it, Paw, a boy or a girl?"

"You got your wish, son. It's a boy. His name is T. J."

Tommy jumped up and down. He knew it, he just knew it. "I have a little brother! Yippee."

* * *

Fall 1923

Tom lay quietly, but wide awake, next to his brothers in the small bed. He couldn't stop shivering. His maw had said it was colder than usual for November, but his quaking was because of the commotion going on in his maw and paw's room.

Once again, he and his siblings were waiting for a new brother or sister. This time it had decided to come in the middle of the night.

T.J. was almost one and a half years old now, and he was already talking good. Tom loved his baby brother, but he was kind of jealous because everyone always talked about how smart T.J. was.

All of Tom's brothers were smart. He was too, but nobody would give him the chance to prove it. According to everyone but his maw, even Mary was smarter than him.

His maw had confidence in him and that had always helped him get past the ribbing. When his paw and brothers were gone on the medicine show that summer, his Maw sometimes played the organ and let him try to strum along on the guitar. He knew a couple of chords already, but someday he'd know them all...someday.

The baby's cry rang out. Tommy squirmed with excitement and wanted to jump out of bed to go find out if it was a girl or boy, but he knew he'd have to wait until morning.

Sleeping was impossible and as soon as the sun rose over the horizon, Tommy was up. He always had to sleep in the middle of Red and Jack. Ike and Bill had their own bed, and Mary got to sleep in their folks' room. He crawled real easy over Red and tiptoed out to the living room.

The smell of coffee in the kitchen told him a grown up was there. He peeked around the corner and saw the midwife standing with her cup in hand. Squaring his shoulders, he entered the room. "Mornin' ma'am."

"Mornin'"

"How's my maw?"

"Oh, she'll be down for a few days 'cause, forty four years is a little old to be havin' babies, but she'll be fine' she smiled and glanced down at him. "You sure are up early."

"Couldn't sleep. Too excited to know if I have a little brother or little sister, ma'am."

She smiled and placed her cup on the counter. Her eyes were kind when she bent down and met his gaze.

"You have a little sister, and her name is Margie. Margie Faye. She's cute as a button."

"A girl! I cain't wait to tell Mary. She'll be so excited she ain't gonna be the only girl anymore. Now me and T.J. won't have to play dolls with her."

"Well, isn't that a nice gift to get for the holidays. Why, Thanksgiving is almost here, and then Christmas is soon to follow."

"I never thought of it that way. A little sister for Christmas." He furrowed his brow. "Ummm, I'd rather have a guitar."

* * *

Music filled the room. It was Christmas day. The Kizziahs had never had a Christmas tree, and this year was no different. Tommy knew they'd be lucky if his folks could even afford a new pair of shoes for each of them.

His baby sister lay on the floor on a pallet made of quilts and Mary was goo-gooing over her, as always. The baby had' been feeling too good lately, she was kind of a weakly little thing, but today she was acting okay.

Aromas of fresh baked pumpkin pie drifted through the house. Even if he never got gifts, his Maw always had a big Christmas dinner. It was the feast of the year at their house and his favorite.

He tapped his foot to the beat and sang along under his breath. Mary was already singing with the family, and she was only six. But that was okay. He just loved being around music. How could Margie sleep through the noise? He guessed that's what babies did best. Sleep.

Between songs, Tommy's mother came from the kitchen, pushing up the hair that had fallen from the bun atop her head. "Lon, the meal's almost ready."

"Okay, Hon. Think we got time for one more song?"

"One more, and that's it."

"Tom, come 'ere, boy."

It took a few seconds to realize his Paw was talking to him. He glanced over at the tall man holding the banjo. "Huh? What? Me, Paw?"

"Ain't your name Tom?"

"Yes, sir, yes sir, it is."

"Well, get over here."

He didn't understand why he was in trouble, but he slowly joined his father and brothers in the corner where they always played.

'T. H., your Maw told me you've been tryin' to sing a little. Play a little guitar, too. Is that right?"

What? He was in trouble for trying to play and sing? He looked up at his Paw.

"Well? Speak up, boy. Is it right?"

"Y-yes, sir," he answered and swallowed hard when his paw took off his banjo. He just knew he was gonna get a thrashin'.

His heart pounded and he fought the urge to run and hide. He'd only had one spanking from his Paw, but that was enough, he didn't want any more. Especially one he didn't do nothing wrong to get!

Stretching to reach way back behind the other instruments, his Paw picked up a guitar Tom had never seen before. He glanced over at his Maw who was smiling. What was going on? He looked back at his Paw.

"It's not brand new, Tom," Lon said. "But it ain't banged up or nothin'."

He couldn't believe his ears. Was his Paw going to give him a guitar? He forced himself to breathe as he listened to the older man strum the strings and make sure they were in tune.

"I got it at the pawn shop in town. The man gave it to me for three dollars." He held the freshly tuned guitar out to his son. "It's all yours, T. H."

Tommy blinked back the tears in his eyes. His brothers would make fun of him if they saw him cry. "Mine, Paw? All mine?" He took the instrument and hoped the smile on his face told his folks how happy he was. His mother's hand was warm on his shoulder.

"You've been wanting that for a long time, T. H. Now you can learn all the songs you want," Janie said.

"That's right," Lon added in a happy, booming voice. He lifted a big box wrapped in plain brown paper. "We got us, right here in this box, a brand new Victrola Phonograph player, y'all. Made by the Victor Talking Machine Company. He pulled the paper off the box and opened it. "This is a gift for the whol' family and there will be no fussin' over it. First time I hear arguin', y'all won't be able to use it anymore. Understand?"

Voices of all pitches, from around the room answered in unison, including Tom's.

"Yes, Paw."

How exciting! He made his way to the couch, careful not to bump his new guitar on anything. The others weren't paying any attention to him. They all wanted to watch their Paw hook up the new phonograph. He, on the other hand, only wanted to play his guitar.

Relaxing back on the cushion he traced the shiny wood with his hand. His Paw really had bought him his own guitar for Christmas. This time he didn't blink back the tears. He allowed them to silently roll down his face and find a resting place on his hand me down shirt. His very own guitar.

* * *

Tommy sat up in bed, startled awake by his mother's worried cries.

"Lon! Lon! There's something wrong with Margie!"

His father's quick, heavy footsteps pounding down the hall matched his own heart's beating! The night's darkness closed in on him and he was more scared than he'd ever been. He'd never heard his maw's voice sound that way before. What was going on?

"Lon, she's rattling in her chest and can't breathe very good. I think we need to get her to the hospital!"

"Okay, you get 'er ready to go and I'll get the car."

The light switch clicked and Tommy squinted against the brightness, but could still see his father standing in the doorway. He looked ten feet tall.

"Ike! Ike!"

Ike sat up and rubbed his eyes. "Yes, Sir?"

"The baby's sick and we're gonna take her to the hospital. You help your maw if she needs ya. I'll meet y'all in front of the house."

Ike got out of bed and slipped on his pants. "Yes, Sir."

Tom couldn't help but ask, "Is Margie going to be okay, Paw?"

"I don't know, T.H.. I just don't know." Lon turned and left the room.

Soon Tommy heard the slamming of the screen door and his mother's instructions for his twenty-year-old brother. He truly hoped Margie would be all right, she was such a sweet baby, but this wasn't the first time she'd been sick, and he knew his folks always worried about her.

He got up, walked up to the doorway and peeked out into the hall. He saw his maw go out the front door with his sister bundled in her arms. There was nothing he could do, so he turned out the light and went back to bed, even though he knew he wouldn't be able to sleep.

Ike came back into the room, took his pants off and lay back down. He was a grown man, but still lived at home and helped take care of the family.

"Ike, I'm scared."

"Don't worry, Tom, they'll take good care of Margie at the hospital. It'll be daylight soon, that'll make ya feel better. Then you can get up, but just lay still and wait for mornin."

He hated waiting, but that's what he did all morning was wait for his folks to come home. Then he heard the car drive up. Rushing to the door, he stopped at the screen and watched his folks get out. Margie wasn't with them.

Slowly, he pushed the door open. By the look on his maw's face and the redness of her eyes, he knew the news wasn't good. "How's the baby, Paw?"

His maw sobbed and his Paw just looked at him with a tear in his eye and shook his head. Tom knew their family had lost one of its members.

Ike sat on the couch. "There's no funeral home here in Dickens Paw. What will we do?"

"We'll burry her in Floydada. That's all we can do, son."

Summer 1924

Tommy placed his fingers on the guitar strings and strummed a chord. He was proud that the first thing he'd done was learn to tune the instrument. His father and brothers now gone on the medicine show left him more time to practice. His goal was to learn enough to be able to go on the show with them next year. He'd be almost ten years old by then and Jack started when he was eight.

The phonograph record sounded like it sizzled when he placed the needle on it, but soon the music would start and he intended to learn every word of the song. Yesterday, he'd learned how to play the tune, bein's he couldn't write, he'd have to play the record over and over again today to learn the words.

The act came naturally to him, and he was surprised that he

only had to listen to the words three times before he remembered them all. He played and sang the song all the way through one more time to make sure he had it right. When he was finished, he yelled into the kitchen, "Hey, Maw, can you come here a minute? I have something to show ya."

His mother ambled into the room wiping her hands on her apron. "What is it Tom. I'm makin' biscuits for supper and I don't want the dough to sit too long."

"Listen, Maw." He strummed the guitar and began to sing words still fresh in him memory. He watched his mother quietly take a seat on the couch. A grin lifted the corners of her mouth while she listened to his music. He pushed the air out of his lungs and held the last note then made the last strum across the strings. He liked having an audience.

"Oh, T.H." She covered her mouth and coughed then continued, "That was beautiful!"

He put his guitar down and felt his cheeks get hot as he looked at the ground. "Thanks, Maw. I just learned it. I'm gonna learn a lot more, Maw. Then I'm going on the medicine show with Paw, if he'll let me." He looked up into his mother's eyes. His heart fell to his belly. She didn't think he was good at all, she thought his performance was terrible. "Maw, why you cryin'?"

She pulled him to her. "I'm just so proud of you, Tom. You've worked so hard, and I'm telling you right now, you can sing the best I ever heard. You're gonna be a star some day. I just know it."

He leaned into his mother's embrace; she always made him feel loved. He could only dream of being a star.

1900 - Teens & Twenty's

Lon Elick
Leonzo
Kizziah

Janie Rebeka
Jane Hickey

Lon & Janie Kizziah

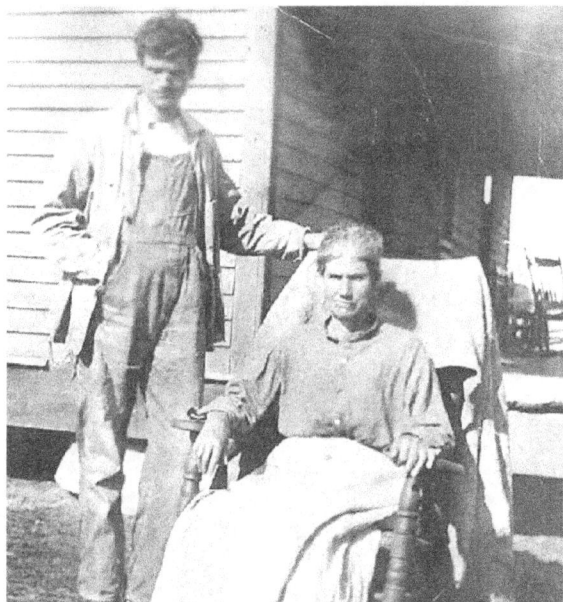

Lydia Hayse Kizziah Jackson
and Lon's brother James

Janie holding baby Tom with Red by her side

Written on the back of the picture by Lon

Top row: Red, Ike & Jack
Sitting: Bill, Lon, Mary, Janie & Tommy

CHAPTER 3

Fall 1924

Tommy blinked back tears as he'd done so many times in the past. Why? Why was he always the one left out? "Mary's gonna get to be on, and I'm not? Why, Maw? I sing as good as she does, and I'm older?"

"T.H., I know you want to be on your daddy's new radio show, and I don't blame you for being upset, but we've got to get to Lubbock. The first show starts today."

"I ain't goin', Maw. There's no need. I'll stay home and listen to the show from here." Her hand was warm under his chin, and she forced him to look at her. He couldn't stop the tears any longer.

"Now, Tom, your day will come. I know it will. It just won't be today. You know I think you're the best, but this is your Paw's show, and he says who's on." She took her hand away and covered her mouth through her coughing spell. When she caught her breath she continued. "Come go with us. It'll be fun. You'll see."

It was true, it would be fun going into a radio station, and he'd never been to Lubbock. Maybe if he went, his paw would change his mind and let him on the show. He took a deep breath and made up his mind. "Okay, Maw, I'll go."

"Good. Now let's get. Everyone's in the car but us."

The ride to Lubbock was uneventful. Everyone practiced their singing parts for the radio show, but Tommy just sat and listened. He could add to the sound, by harmonizing, but he didn't even try. When he asked his paw one last time if he could join them on the show, he flatly said no.

He didn't want to push it. His feelings were hurt enough and he wasn't going to give anyone a chance to do it more. Bill was seventeen years old now, and didn't rib him too much, but Jack was fourteen, Red was eleven and they both liked to give him heck about anything they could.

Finally they reached a tall building. "This is it, y'all," Lon said. "You boys get the instruments out of the trunk, then I'll park the car."

They all piled out. Tom missed the truck. At least they could ride in the back and he didn't feel like he was squashed in a can of sardines. But the truck broke down, and this was what his Paw bought.

"Hey, Jack, let me get Paw's guitar, okay?"

"Sure, Tom, here." Jack handed him the case. "Just wait right inside the door there."

His pulse thumped. A real, live radio station. Man, he could' believe it. And he was about to see it. "Okay, Jack."

He smiled and carried the guitar case inside the tall building. He glanced around. He didn't see anything that looked like a radio station to him. Maybe they were in the wrong place.

The door opened and the rest of his family entered. "Hey, Paw, I don't see no radio station."

"That's because it's on the third floor, T.H. We have to take the elevator."

"Wow, I ain't never been on an elevator before."

A man inside the thing they called an elevator had on a funny suit. He pulled the gate shut and turned a lever.

It felt like they zoomed up and Tommy almost lost his stomach. What a ride!

"This is it." Lon said as the door opened.

Everyone stepped out, but when Tommy tried to get out, his

paw stopped him.

"T.H., you stay on the elevator. This man here will take care of you."

"But why, Paw?"

"Lon, what are you doing?" Janie asked.

"Hon, we cain't have Tom going in the radio station."

"And why not?"

"I know it sounds awful, but people will be starin' at him because of his eye."

"You ca' be serious."

"I'm sorry, but I am. Now let's go." He took Janiee's arm. "Tom, the show is only fifteen minutes long and it is going to start soon, so we won't be long. You just stay here and be good."

Tommy didn't fight the tears this time, he could'. He'd never felt this way before. It was something in his chest, kind of the same thing that happened when Margie died.

"But, Paw…"

"No buts T.H. You mind me."

Janie jerked her arm away from her husband's grasp. "If Tom doesn't go, I don't either." She turned on her heels and got back on the elevator. "We'll be in the car."

"Suit yourself," Lon said, and walked away.

The door slid shut and Janie handed Tommy her handkerchief. "I'm so sorry T.H. I didn't know your paw was going to do that, or I would' have talked you into coming along."

"It's not your fault, Maw. It's mine for being so ugly. Paw's never liked me because of my eye."

She bent down and took him by the shoulders. "Now don't you say your Paw don't like you. Why, he loves you, Tom. He just don't know how to handle things sometimes. I love you, too. And you're not ugly. You're the best looking boy I've got. We're gonna get you some eye glasses one of these days, and you'll see, when that eye is straightened up, you'll be handsome as all get out."

The door slid open and daylight streamed through the windows of the front of the building. "Let's get out of this musty ol' place and get us some fresh air. My lungs are begging for it."

He saw her try to stifle a cough, but it made its way to the surface just as they left the building. "Maw, your coughin's gettin' worse again."

"I know it, son, but don't you worry about it. I'll be fine."

He hoped so. She was the only one who believed in him.

Wiping the last of the tears from his face, he promised himself he'd never cry again from getting his feelings hurt. That was for babies and he was a big boy.

Big enough that he knew he was gonna be the best of them all. He'd learn every song he could and he'd have his own radio show someday. They could just watch and see.

* * *

Spring 1928

"I'm sorry you're sick, Maw, but do we really have to move to Oklahoma?" Tommy again noticed how gaunt his mother's face looked and knew he'd asked a dumb question.

"Your Paw, Jack and Red already have a job there working for the railroad. Besides, El Reno is close to the town that the TB sanitarium's in, T.H. You'll like it there, too." A deep cough racked her lungs.

"Yeah, I guess. Maw, what exactly is Tuberculosis anyway?"

"It's a lung disease. I guess I've had it for a good while, T.H. We just didn't know what it was. I'll get to that sanitarium and maybe I'll get well, but right now, you need to help me pack these things up, or we'll never get there.

Tommy glanced at his guitar sitting in the corner. He longed to go and play it, but now he had to help his mother.

"Maw, I bought me a new phonograph record the other day with the money I made helpin' Mr. Tummons. I like it a lot and

I've almost got it learned already."

"I've never seen anybody as good at learning things by ear, Tom. You are so smart."

"Thanks, Maw, it just kinda happens. A guy named Jimmy Rogers is singin' it and it's called Sleep, Baby, Sleep. The one on the other side's called The Soldier's Sweetheart. I'm gonna learn that, too. Soon as we get moved and all."

"We'll be moved in less then a week. I'm gonna miss Ike. He's decided to go on to Oklahoma City to live. Thankfully TJ and Mary's stay in the city will be short. And now that Bill has married that nice girl Virgie, he wouldn't be going. I'm surprised Jack isn't staying behind to marry Jessie Suggs, too.

"My babies are all gonna be leaving me soon. Everybody growin' up and all. We'll miss Ike's and Bill's income, too, but Jack and Red will be helping out. So, you'll have plenty of time to learn your songs."

"I'll do some work, too, Maw. I can help."

"I know you will, Tom, but you're the best singer in the family and I want you to keep doing that.

"I'll do that, too. I really like Jimmy Rogers' singin'. I've never heard anybody that good. Cept me." He looked at his maw and began to laugh at his own funny. She started to laugh too, but began to cough. It was a bad one and Tommy could' do anything for her, no matter how much he wanted to. Through her labored breathing she struggled to speak.

"Say, why don't you take a break and sing the new tune for me."

"Really, Maw?"

"Sure. Matter of fact, I'm going to take a break too and sit right there on the couch and listen."

Happy to let her rest, he picked up the guitar, made sure it was in tune, then began his performance to his favorite audience. His mother. She was really the only audience he'd ever had, besides his little brothers and sister, but they didn't really care. His Maw was his biggest fan and he loved her.

"And now, ladies and gentleman, from the stage at the Kizziah house I'd like to sing for ya, Sleep, Baby, Sleep by Jimmy Rogers." He liked puttin' on a little show, and his maw always seemed to enjoy it.

He took a deep breath and began the song. Janie tapped her foot to the tune. It had been a long time since she'd gotten to sing and he wondered if she missed it as much as he knew he would if he didn't get to do it.

His mother's applause always pleased him. "Thank ya, folks. Thank ya, very much. Would ya like to hear another one?"

"I would, but I guess we'd better get back to work."

"Okay, Maw." He put the guitar back and stopped to face her. "Maw, I was wonderin', what is Paw gonna do with the little ones when you're in the sanitarium?"

"Nig is going to stay with the James' in Oklahoma City. But it's for temporary, just till we get settled, then we'll bring him to El Reno."

"I've always wondered why you call T.J., Nig."

She smiled. "I don't know. I guess it's because of that silly song he sings sometimes. He's my little Nig, that's all."

She didn't want to leave her baby behind, he could tell. Heck, he was twelve years old now, he knew a lot of things. One thing he knew for sure was that he'd miss his mother something terrible while she was in the sanitarium.

They'd be living in a new town, a new house and she would' be there. He hoped she'd get to come home soon. Mary was the only girl in the family, and she was staying in Oklahoma City with some friends.

* * *

It was strangely quiet in the new house without Ike, Bill, Mary and T.J. there. T.J. was seven now, and would be better off with the McKinnon's in Rosebud, Texas. Maybe that way he'd be lucky and get some schoolin'. Mary was ten and would probably get some education, too, be'ins she was going to live with the James' in Chandler, Oklahoma. He'd been surprised when Bill announced he'd be movin' to Mineral Wells, Texas. He had a friend there and this seemed like a good time to get on with his life. Heck, Bill was twenty years old.

His brothers were growin' up. His family was falling apart and there was' anything he could do about it.

Tommy missed his maw already and she'd only left for the sanitarium in Clinton, Oklahoma, that morning. She was' doin' too good and that worried him, but he had his music as a comfort.

He'd worked hard at learning songs and it had paid off. His Paw told him that he could go with them on the medicine show that summer. That is, if his Paw could find a local show that needed them.

Tommy knew the change of heart was because in the last few months his cocked eye seemed to be getting better. It still was' down all the way, and he could' see good out of it, but it looked better anyway.

It could be, too, that he had to go because his mother would' be there to watch him and Red, but they were big enough now, they didn't need anybody to look after them. He didn't care, at least he would be performing for people and that was his dream. He only hoped a show in the area needed them.

Red ran through the door in a fury. "Hey, Tom, guess what?"

He'd never seen his freckled faced brother so excited. "What?"

"I get to go on the medicine show, too. Paw said I could."

"But, Red, you don't sing or nothin'."

"I know, but I'm gonna take care of the instruments and stuff like that. Won't it be fun, Tom?"

His fifteen-year-old brother was more excited than he'd ever seen. He thought about standing in front of all those people and for a moment his stomach had butterflies. Could he do it? He nodded his head. "Yeah, it'll be real fun."

Jack's voice rang through the screen door. "Tom, come out here."

Red ran ahead of him and jumped off the porch, happy in his own little world. "Yeah, what is it, Jack?" Tom asked.

"Paw said you had to mow the yard today. He bought a new mower just for you."

"Oh, just what I've always wanted." He hoped the flat tone of his voice told his brother he was' thrilled. "A lawn mower. Does it have a motor on it?"

"Nope, just a push mower with blades on it."

"How'd I know that?"

"Oh, stop snivelin' and start mowin'. It looks like it might be comin' up a storm and Paw wants it done today."

"Okay, okay." He started to walk away and felt Jack's hand on his shoulder.

"T.H."

What now? "Huh?"

"Paw found a medicine show for us."

His heart jumped to his throat and he looked into his older brother's eyes. No wonder Red was so excited. He knew about it already. "Really?"

"Yep. It only travels around here close, so we can come home often, and go see Maw. We leave next week, that's why Paw wants to get this place into shape before we go."

"Yiiiiippppppeeeee. I really get to go on a show." He wrapped his arms around Jack and gave him the biggest hug he could muster. "Thanks, Jack."

"Welcome. Now go get started on this lawn."

"Yes, Sir!"

He made his way to the shed and got out the shiny new mower. How could something that made you do so much work be so pretty? It would' take long for it to get dirty as he did his job today.

Surprised at how easy it was to push in the tall grass, Tom let his mind wander. Really, his paw didn't have to take him on the medicine show. Red was old enough to watch after him at home. He lifted the corners of his mouth into a wide grin and spoke to a butterfly that flew by, "He doesn't have to take me, he wants me to go."

* * *

"Tom, we need to get to practicin' now, so come on in here."

"I'm comin', Paw." Tommy grabbed his guitar and hurried from the bathroom into the living room to join his family band. He was all fluttery inside and had to pee. He guessed he was just too excited.

Lon pointed to an empty space between him and Jack. "Stand right there, son, and we'll get started."

He took his place and listened for further instructions.

"I'll be playin' banjo now since Bill's gone, Jack'll still play fiddle and the guitar parts will be all yours. You already know all the songs we do, don't ya, T.H.?"

"Yes, Sir."

"Then I guess we'll be learnin' the ones you know, so you're in charge of this practice session."

Tommy swallowed hard. He'd never been in charge of nothin' in his life. His mind was blank, where would he start? Silence filtered through the room as his brother and paw waited for his instructions.

"Tom, you in there, boy? We're waitin'."

"Oh, yeah, a-ah sure, Paw." He stood up tall and inhaled a deep breath. It was now or never. He cleared his throat and the words seemed to boom from deep inside his chest, "This one's in the key of C. It's the newest Jimmy Rogers song called Blue Yodel - T-for Texas and it goes like this."

He thumped out the first three notes on his guitar leading into the song..."T for Texas, T for Tennessee...T for Texas, T for Tennessee...T for Thelma, gal sure made a wreck outta' me."

The others picked right up on the chord progression of all the songs he did, and Tommy tried to hide his disappointed when his Paw said they could quit for the evening. He could go on all night long. "Paw, that was fun. How'd I do?"

"You did real good, T.H. Better than I expected. Just like your maw said, you're a natural." He ruffled Tom's black wavy hair. "I'm proud of ya. You took over like a professional. You're gonna add a lot, T.H. I'm sorry I didn't let you go before now, when Bill was still with us."

Was his dad trying to apologize to him? "Ah, that's okay, Paw, I understand."

"Well, it was wrong of me to leave you out all them years, but you're part of us now, and I'm glad."

Oh, no, he could' cry! Pride welled up in his heart and he turned away so his Paw would' see it if he did tear up. "I'm glad, too, Paw."

If his paw never came any closer to telling him he loved him, that was just fine with him. At least deep down inside he knew he could carry the knowledge with him the rest of his life.

* * *

"Pack 'er up real good there, Red. We don't want any of those tonic bottles to get broke."

"Okay, Paw. I'm doin' it good, just like ya told me to."

Tom walked to the old, small trailer Red was helping to load. He set his guitar down. They didn't have that much stuff, but it was more than would fit in the trunk of the car. "Hey, Red, see the new case Paw got for my guitar? Well, it's not really new, he bought it at the pawn shop, but it will protect it anyway."

"Yeah, Tom, that's real nice. Hand it here, I got just the place for it."

He picked it up. "Now you be careful with it." He handed it to his brother.

"I will Tom, I will. If I let somethin' happen to this stuff, Paw would skin me alive! And I kinda like my ol' freckled skin."

Tom joined in Red's laughter. He could' remember ever being this happy and excited. He only wished his maw could be there to share it with him. He'd got to go visit her last week and she looked bad. Really bad.

He'd never talked to God much, but his Maw asked him to, so he was sure to talk to Him every day about making her better.

"Well, that's it, boys. We're all loaded up and ready to go," Lon said.

Red looked down in his own little shy way. "did I do good, Paw?"

Lon inspected the work. "I'd say you did a fine job, Red. Fine indeed."

The redhead shot Tommy a sideways glance and a grin.

"Now, let's get to it. Our first show's tonight and we got a few miles to go. I hope the place will be okay while we're gone. We'll be home in about two weeks."

Jack got to sit in the front seat while Tom and Red sat in the back. Tommy looked out the back glass as they pulled away from the house. He watched the old wooden trailer sway back and forth as it followed.

Usually all the folks on the show traveled together, but this time, his paw explained, they were all gonna meet up at the first show stop, then go on together from there. He could' wait to meet the other folks on the show. He liked to laugh at the slapstick comedians and watch all the stuff the other perform-ers did, but fellow musicians were going to be his favorite. Why, no tellin' what he could learn from them.

He leaned back in the seat. Tonight was the night. He'd be in front of a live audience for the very first time. All of a sud-den, he realized this is what he'd been dreaming of since he was a little boy. Now he was almost a teenager and it was real-ly happening. His dream was coming true. He rested his head against the back of the seat, closed his eyes and his voice was just above a whisper, "Thank you, God."

"We're here!"

His Paw's voice startled him. He must have fallen asleep. Wow, that made the trip go by really fast. He'd have to do that every time, then they'd be there before he knew it.

"Let's get this stuff out and all set up, boys. The show starts in just an hour."

Tom wished he could have one of the sandwiches they'd brought, but there'd be plenty of time to eat when they were done settin' up. He was hungry, but with all the flutterin' his stomach was doin' he was' even sure he could get a sandwich down!

"Tom, put that right over there. Red, set that here." His Paw's voice vibrated with authority.

"I think that's all of it, Paw."

Lon glanced at the set up. "I guess that'll do, then. Now when I start hawkin' the tonic, you boys grab those bottles as fast as you can and push 'em to the people. Be sure and get their money. That's what we're here for, to get these folks' money, T.H."

Tommy looked up to meet his father's gaze. "Yes, Sir?"

"Think you know your numbers good enough to do this?"

"Yes, Sir. Jack's been showin' us what to do and how to make change. I think I can do it, Paw."

"Good enough. We're gonna start in just a little bit, so if y"all are hungry, now's the time to grab a bite."

A tall lanky young man approached them. "Hey, Lon, you got new helpers on this trip?"

Lon offered a handshake and smiled. "Greasy! Dad-gum-it, what are you doing in these parts? Are you on the show?"

"Sure 'nuff. I got me a new partner."

"He's the straight man, ain't he?"

Greasy cocked one eyebrow. "Course, you know nobody's as funny as me."

Lon shook his head. "Gotta be the truth, Grease. Hey, let me introduce ya to our newest member and our new, well I guess you'd call him our packer-upper. Tom, this is Greasy. He's one of our slapstickers."

He stuck out his hand and accepted the young man's shake. "Nice to meet ya. Don't think I've ever known nobody named Greasy before."

"And probably never will again, Tom," Greasy said.

"This here's Red. He's the only one of my kids that has freckles. Took after his Maw, I guess."

"Howdy, Red."

Red kicked at the ground and Tommy punched him. "Shake his hand, goofy."

His brother raised his hand without raising his head. "Howdy."

"Well, Greasy, it's good to see ya, boy. I'm glad you're on the show, but me and the boys better get us a bite before the show starts."

"Okay, Lon, I'll be seein' ya. Nice to meet ya fellas," Greasy said as he walked away.

Tommy listened to his Paw's words about food, and watched his brothers head for the car, but he could'. Hungry as he was, he was in awe watching the people gather. In a few minutes, he would be part of a full-fledged medicine show and would be playing music for them all. Would they like him? Would they clap for him the same as his maw did?

His maw. He wished she was there to calm him down. She always had a way of makin' things easier, and he sure could use a big ol' hug 'bout right now. He shook his head and frowned. What the heck was he thinkin'? Hells bells, he was almost a teenager and wantin' his maw. Man, if his brothers knew what he was thinkin' they'd call him a sissy or some-thin'. His Paw's voice rang through his thoughts.

"Let's play!"

Tommy's heart skipped a beat and he whispered, "Time to

grow up."

He grabbed his guitar and took his place on the small stage between his paw and Jack. He played a couple of chords, his paw plunked on his banjo, and Jack sawed a few notes on his fiddle. Sure they were in tune, his Paw stepped toward the people congregated in front.

"Howdy, folks! We're the Kizziah's and we're here to make ya feel better. We're gonna play some music for ya now. My boy Tom will be singin' the first number. T for Texas. Tom?"

First! He was gonna be first? His feet were filled with lead and he could' step to the front of the stage, but Jack gave him a little push and he moved past his Paw. Surely his heart was going to come through his chest it was beating so hard, and he had to pee, but he knew that was' possible. His Paw's voice came from behind.

"Okay, kick 'er off, Jack."

He swallowed the lump in his throat, and it was the first time in his life he was glad he could' see that good. Not bein' able to see the people's faces clear made it easier. When it was time, his mouth flew open and the words spilled out just like he knew what he was doin'. "T for Texas...T for Tennessee."

It felt great! And sounded good, too. When the song was over the crowd burst into applause louder than any he'd ever heard, and it was for him and his family. Pride welled up inside as he stepped back and took his place again. At that moment he knew, music would be his life.

CHAPTER 4

Fall 1929

Tommy was a teenager now and it was his second summer on the Medicine show. His Maw was still in the sanitarium. He couldn't believe almost two years had passed since she'd gone in.

They went back to Texas a couple of times to see T.J. and Mary, but his Paw couldn't bring the little ones back without his Maw being home. And the way things looked, she wouldn't ever be home again.

Along with their Paw, he, Jack and Red sat quietly on the front steps of the big red bricked building waiting to get in to see their mother.

He heard the door behind them squeak and turned to see a gray haired man in a white jacket come out. He pulled a cloth mask that was tied around his head off his nose and let it rest around his neck.

His Paw stood and greeted him. "Howdy, Doc. I got your message and I brought the boys like you suggested."

"She's really bad, Lon. Are you sure you want them to see her this way."

Tommy stepped up. "I wanna see 'er, Paw. I haven't seen 'er in a spell, and if this might be the last time, I don't care how bad she is, I wanna see 'er."

"How 'bout you boys?"

His brothers nodded. "See, Paw, we all want to see her."

The doctor ran his fingers through his hair. "Okay, Lon, I'll go and get her. Now mind you, she's very thin. She don't look like she did even the last time you saw her. I won't be able to get her in a wheel chair, she's too frail, but her bed has rollers on it, so I'll bring her out of the quarantined part of the sanitarium and put her in a private room where y'all can be alone. Here's you some masks. Put them on and y'all can go inside to the waiting room. You don't have to sit out here."

"All right, we'll come in. When you're ready, doc, just point the way."

The sadness in his paw's voice was evident, and Tommy knew it was almost over for his maw.

Cool, dry air came in, and hot, moist air went out as he breathed through the cloth. He sat in the soft cushioned chair and thought of all the wonderful things she'd done for him. Her support of his music, telling him he was handsome when everybody else said he was ugly, standing up for him with his paw...He couldn't begin to name all the things.

The almost two years that had gone by without her home. Every minute had been hard, but it also forced him to grow. She'd be worried about him and how he'd get along in life, but he'd make it just fine.

"She's ready," the doctor announced. "Now remember, she's very weak, so don't feel bad if she don't say much."

He was the first to stand up. His paw and brothers followed. "Can we see her one at a time, or do we have to go in all at once?"

"Which ever way y'all want to do it'll be fine, son," the doctor replied, then turned to lead them down the hall.

His Paw walked just behind the doctor. Jack, Red and he followed. He wanted to spend some time alone with his maw, even if it were only a minute. He had to tell her something he'd wanted to tell her for a long time. "Paw?"

His paw turned toward him. "Yeah, T.H."

"I want to see Maw by myself, if that's okay."

"It's okay, son, but why don't you come in with us, and we'll all see 'er together, then we'll take turns being alone with 'er."

He nodded in agreement and followed along. When they entered the room, it smelled clean, but musty. He looked at his poor sickly mother and wanted to run. He'd never seen anyone look so bad. There was no meat on her bones and she was pale with dark circles around her eyes.

Bile rose in his throat and threatened to spill on the floor, but he swallowed hard to push it down. This was for sure the last time he'd see his maw. She was gonna die.

He stood back and didn't say a word, but watched as his brothers said their goodbyes and was surprised to see tears streaming down each of their faces. He didn't think they could love her as much as he did, but he guessed they did. He'd never seen any of them cry before, 'cept Red, but he could tell their hearts were breaking, just like his.

His paw spoke softly. "Janie, Ike couldn't come from Oklahoma City, but he wanted me to tell ya he got married a couple of months ago to a real nice girl named Thelma. They're doin' okay, but don't have the money to visit. Bill's still in Mineral Wells, and he's doin' good, too.

His Maw's voice was so faint he could hardly hear what she said.

"What about Nig and Mary?"

"Nig's still in Texas and Mary's in Chandler. They're in school, getting an education like you wanted and gonna grow up to be good folks.

Still in the background, Tommy waited a long while, then his mother's voice seemed to get stronger, and her words rang deep in his heart.

"I'm gonna die, boys."

Her cough racked her lungs, but it was the weakest cough he'd ever heard. When the spell was over, he listened hard so he could capture every word.

"That's all there is to it. I want you all to know how proud I am of you, and you're all special to me in your own way. I just wish I was gonna get to see all of my children grow up. But no matter, I'll be with God and I'll be watching over y'all wherever you are." She tried to lift her head, but couldn't. "Where's T.H., Lon?"

"He's here, Hon, he wants to be alone with you, so he's waiting his turn."

A weak smile touched her lips. "I think it's gonna be soon, Lon, so I'd better talk to him now."

"Okay, Hon." He kissed his wife on the forehead and said, "We'll be right outside the door. I'll let you talk to T.H. then I'll come back in."

She nodded a silent okay, and Tommy watched his brothers go by and give her a last goodbye hug. Red cried the worst and he was surprised to see his Paw's arm around Red's shoulder as they left the room.

Tommy pushed the door shut and stepped up to his maw's bedside. He fought back the tears that wanted to fall. He wouldn't let his mother see him cry.

"My gosh, T.H., you've grown up overnight!"

Her frail voice was like music to his ears. "Thanks, Maw."

He looked at her tiny little hands and remembered how strong they used to be. He grasped one with his, and wiped the stray hair from her face. Her hair had some white in it, but other than that, it was the only thing about her that hadn't changed.

"I hate to leave you alone, son."

He smiled the most confident smile he could muster. "It's okay, Maw, I'm gonna be fine, and it's all because of you. You taught me to be strong, and that's just what I'm gonna be." He wanted her to believe that, so he continued to blink back his tears.

"I'm glad to hear it."

"Maw, I want to tell ya somethin' before you go to meet the Maker."

"What is it?"

He cleared his throat and looked straight into her faded hazel eyes. "I love you, Maw. I love you more than I'll ever love anyone in the world. You're my best friend, and I'm gonna miss ya, but you and God are gonna get along just fine up there, and I know you'll be my guardian angel." He wiped a tear from her cheek. "Go on and rest, Maw, you've suffered enough."

She gave a slight nod, closed her eyes and silent tears wet her pillow.

He pulled the mask away, lifted her hand to his mouth and pressed his lips to her soft skin. When he laid her arm back on the bed, she opened her eyes and looked at him.

"I love you, too, T.H., and you're right, I will be your guardian angel."

* * *

At the graveside, Tommy stood beside his brothers. The preacher had talked and everyone left but them. He was sorry his Grandma Lyd couldn't come, but money was scarce and it was a long way to Tennessee. He was also disappointed Ike couldn't get there.

As reality of losing a loved one set in, he wondered if he'd ever see Grandma Lydia again. Probably not, she'd been old when they left Rockwood and that was years ago.

A man walked by and soon he heard the thud of dirt landing on top of his mother's casket. Someone tugged on his shirt and he glanced up at his Paw.

"Let's go, T.H. We'll let these fellas bury your Maw now."

Tommy picked up a handful of dirt and threw it in the hole, then turned and followed his family. His Mother was gone, and he had accepted that he'd never see his favorite fan again. Her support had meant everything to him, but now he'd have to stiffen his backbone and become a man. He was bound and determined to do it, too. She was watching over him just like

Letter from Tommy's Grandmother Lydia after Janie's death.

found left Saturday
evening + break his
ankle bone he is in
the hospital at
Rockwood Son I wish
I could have come
out there but of
course I couldn't.
I hope you + the
children can get
along all right
Son write me soon
your mother
Lydia Jackson

she said she would. He could feel her lending him her strength.

When they got back to the house, he turned on the radio and tuned it to an Oklahoma City station. He couldn't believe his ears when he heard the announcer's voice. He felt the message was sent from his maw.

"That's right, folks, The Blue Yodeler himself, Jimmy Rogers, is going to be right here in Oklahoma City for the next sixteen weeks. He'll be performing in a theater down town five nights a week, and he'll be doing a radio show right here on our station Monday through Saturday. We invite you to listen in at one o'clock every afternoon for fifteen minutes of Mr. Rogers' music."

How exciting! Jimmy Rogers was just a hop, skip and a jump away. Right in OK City! "Paw, Paw, did you hear that?"

"Hear what, T.H.?"

"The radio man."

"Oh, sorry, son, I wasn't listenin'."

"He said Jimmy Rogers is in Oklahoma City. Can we go, Paw? Can we go?"

"We ain't got the money to go, Son. I wish we could. I know you like that man's music."

"Like it. He's my favorite, Paw. I got four dollars I can chip in."

"T.H. I don't wanna hear no more about it. We cain't go. Over, done!"

He couldn't blame his paw for bein' in a foul mood. Maybe he'd wait a couple of days and ask again. Let his maw's death settle a bit.

The more he thought about havin' a chance to see Jimmy Rogers in person, the more excited he got. The real guy. Tommy wished he could sing for the man. Show him how many of his songs he knew by heart.

When he went to bed that night, he said a prayer, goodnight to his maw and drifted off to dream of possibly meeting

Jimmy Rogers.

Morning came and Tommy couldn't wait a couple more days to ask his paw again about going to Oklahoma City. He traipsed through the house, but couldn't find him. Finally he saw his brother. "Jack, where's Paw?"

He went to Chandler to see Mary, Tom. He wanted to give her some of Maw's things. He's gonna be gone for a few days."

A few days? Hells bells, he couldn't wait a few days. He wanted to go to Oklahoma City now! His mind went in circles. What was he gonna do? Jack could drive, but if his paw took the car, Jack couldn't take him. He probably wouldn't anyway. The only other thing he could do was walk. That's it. He'd walk. Even better, he'd put his thumb out and maybe someone would give him a ride.

Man alive, his paw was gonna wallop him, but he couldn't help it. Something was calling him, and he figured since his maw was his guardian angel, she'd watch after him. Maybe even keep him from a beatin'.

After a quick bath, he found his best shirt and the only pair of overalls he had that didn't have holes in them. It was already eight o'clock in the morning so he'd have to hurry. Maybe he could get there before the one o'clock show and get to see Mr. Rogers today!

He picked up his guitar case and walked out the front door. Jack and Red were sitting on the porch and Jack was practicing his fiddle.

"Where ya goin', Tom?" Red asked.

"To Oklahoma City to meet Jimmy Rogers."

Jack put down the instrument. "How you gonna get there?

"Hitchhike."

"You cain't do that. Paw'll kill you for runnin' off."

"I ain't runnin' off. I'll get back in a couple of days. I'm just gonna meet him and sing for him if I can."

"So, what do you think he's gonna do? Give you a job singin' in his band." Jack elbowed Red and the two laughed.

They could make fun all they wanted, but he was doin' this. "I ain't lookin' for no job. I just want to meet him, that's all. Hopefully I'll be back before Paw."

"Like he ain't gonna know you went?"

"He'll know, but maybe he won't be so mad if I'm back before him."

"Whatever you think, T.H., but I wouldn't want to be in your shoes when he finds out."

Red shook his head. "Me neither!"

"Well, I'll be seein' y'all." He turned and started to walk away.

Jack stood. "Hey, Tommy."

He faced his brother once again. "Yeah?"

"You got any money?"

"Four dollars."

Jack dug into his pocket. "Here, I have six, that'll give you ten. You be careful, and if you need us find a telephone and call over to the hardware store where I've been workin'. Mr. Tillman will come get me. I got the number right here. He gave it to me on a piece of paper yesterday."

He took the money and the number and put them in the breast pocket of his overalls. "Thanks, Jack."

Red stepped up and in his shy way said, "If I had any money, I'd give it to ya, too, Tom. Why, I guess you're just about the best sanger I ever heard. Somebody needs to hear ya besides those folks that come to the shows to get drunk on the tonic we sell."

He couldn't stop the laugh that fought its way out. It was true. The tonic did make everyone feel pretty good. Even if they didn't ever say it, he knew his two brothers loved him, and he did them, too. "Thanks, Red. I'll be back before ya know it."

Guitar in hand, he headed for the highway that led to Oklahoma City. It wasn't too far. His thoughts went back to his mother, his sister and little brother. He missed them, but was bound and determined to go on with his life. Before he knew it, he was at the Oklahoma City cut off.

Car's whizzed by. He stayed off the pavement and walked in the brown grass. He'd feel silly sticking his thumb out, but he wanted to get there in a hurry, so he took a chance. One car passed, then another and another. So many passed, he couldn't count, but he couldn't give up. He wanted to see Mr. Rogers today. He only wished he had a watch so he'd know what time it was. By the looks of the sun, it was about ten in the morning. Hells bells, he had to hurry.

Would a little prayer help? It couldn't hurt. Dear Lord, I know this is a dumb thing to ask, but please, help me get a ride. If you cain't do it, would you ask my maw to? Thanks, Lord.

At least ten more cars passed in the next little while. He was about to give in to the thought that it would be tomorrow before he got to see Jimmy Rogers, when an old man in a pickup, about as old, stopped.

"You need a ride?"

"Yes, sir, I do."

"What's that in the case?"

"My guitar."

"Can you play it?"

What did he mean, could he play it? "Course."

"Then take it outta the case, put the case in the back, get in and play me a tune."

"Is it gonna cost me any money for the ride?"

"Nope, just a song or two."

What luck! Guitar in hand, he placed the case in the back of the truck and jumped into the cab. "How far you goin', mister?"

"I'm goin' to Ok City to visit my boy. Where you goin'?"

"I'm goin' to the city, too. I'm gonna sing for Jimmy Rogers."

"Ya, don't say, now." He revved up the motor and pulled onto the pavement. "Well, why don't you show me your stuff?"

Tommy smiled. "Yes, Sir."

* * *

The buildings towered over them in some areas of Oklahoma City. Tommy felt free for the first time in his life. He was doing exactly what he wanted to do, and all by himself. Well, with the help of the old man that picked him up.

"Accordin' to the directions we got from them folks a while ago, that should be the radio station right there."

Finally. Surely it was too late. "What time is it?"

The old man took out his pocket watch and glanced at it. "Bout 12:30."

He'd made it and had thirty minutes to spare. Thank ya, Lord. His heart thumped when they stopped in front of the red brick building. It wasn't as big as some of the others, and not fancy at all, but the call letters of the station were posted on the front and he knew they were at the right place.

"Well, I guess this is it, boy. You sing real good for Mr. Rogers just like you did for me. You have talent, that's for sure." He stuck out his hand for a shake. "Nice to meet ya, ah, what'd you say your name is?"

He grasped the man's hand. "Thomas Henry Kizziah, and yours?"

"Harold. Just plain ol' Harold."

Guitar in hand, he stepped out of the truck. "Thank ya for the ride, Harold."

"You're welcome, Tom."

After shutting the truck door, he grabbed his case out of the back and stuck his head back through the open window. "Do I owe you anything, Harold?"

"Nope, just like I said, you paid me with them songs you sung. And damn good-'un's, too."

Tommy grinned, tapped the side of the truck and stepped away when the old man drove off. For some reason, he thought he was gonna miss the old codger. Harold treated him like a man, not a boy, and he liked it. He only hoped Mr. Rogers would see him in the same light.

He took a deep breath and stepped up on the curb. This was it, his chance to meet his idol. He put the case down, placed the guitar in it and moved toward the wooden door with a window in it. When he stepped inside the building there were a few people milling around, and one really pretty lady sitting at a desk with a telephone on the wall beside her.

Running his fingers through his hair to try to calm the waves, he approached her. "Howdy, ma'am."

"Hi, what can I do for you, young man?"

He set his guitar case down. "I'd like to see Mr. Jimmy Rogers."

She glanced at the clock. "He has a radio show in about twenty minutes. I'm not sure if he'll have time to see you. You might have to wait until he's done."

"Oh, please, can you just ask him? I won't take up much of his time. I just want to sing him a song, that's all."

Her pretty features softened. "Well, all right, I'll go see. You wait here."

He forced down the lump in his throat. He hadn't even been that nervous the first time he sang at the medicine show. Hopefully, his voice wouldn't crack or make some kind of stupid noise when he tried to use it. Seconds seemed like hours but then the lady came back.

She pointed to a chair. "You can have a seat right over there. He'll be out shortly."

His heart skipped a beat. "Really?"

"Really," she said and took her seat again.

He wasn't sure his legs would carry him across the room, but he made the effort and before he could sit down, he heard a man's voice.

"Is this him?"

"Yes, Mr. Rogers, it is."

Surly his heart wasn't going to stop beating right then and there. He turned and met the gaze of the man he recognized from pictures he'd seen of him. Funny, he seemed thinner in real life, and Tommy was almost as tall as him.

He put out his hand and tried to stop it from trembling. "Mr. Rogers, my name's Tom and I'm here to sing for ya."

The man's smile was warm. He was a real person after all.

"Howdy, boy, you can call me Jimmy."

CHAPTER 5

Jimmy Rogers laughed when Tommy finished his song. He was crushed. Mr. Rogers must have thought it was awful and was going to make fun of him.

"Wanda!"

The girl at the desk turned her attention to Jimmy. "Sir?"

"This boy's great! I want him on the show...today."

What? Were his ears playing tricks on him? Jimmy Rogers liked his singin'!

"But Jimmy, the program is almost ready to start."

"That's okay, he can sing the song he just sang for me. It is one of mine."

Tommy had to pee. He wasn't going to be able to hold it, he just knew it.

"Boy, bring your guitar and follow me."

He stood. "Mr. Rog-Rogers, ah," Oh, god, he was gonna wet his pants before he got the words out.

"What is it, boy, come on, we got a show to do."

He cleared his throat. "Ah, sir, I-I need to pee first." Laughter filled the room. Everyone was looking at him, but he'd rather they know he had to go because he told 'em, than to know because he peed his pants.

Jimmy put his arm around Tom's shoulder. "Okay, sonny, the bathroom's on the way to the studio. Let's go."

The bathroom door squeaked open and he handed Jimmy his guitar case. Was this really happening? Was he really going to sing on a live radio show with Jimmy Rogers?

Damn, he wondered if his paw'd be listenin', and how bad he'd skin 'im for walkin' off like that. Oh, well, wasn't anything he could do about it now. Maybe he'd get lucky and his paw'd be proud of him.

He flushed the fancy toilet and hurried to join the older man waiting in the hallway. "Mr. Rogers, I cain't thank ya enough for lettin' me be on your show. I wasn't expectin' this."

"What were you expecting when you walked through that door, sonny?"

What was he expectin? "I don't rightly know, sir. I just wanted to sing for ya, that's all."

They entered a small room. A man was sitting at a work area that had some kind of gadget with more knobs than he'd ever seen, two phonograph turntables, a microphone, the chair the man was sitting in and an extra chair. He gently ran his hand across the phonograph records that lined the back wall of the small enclosure. Why, he'd give his right arm to have that many records.

"Better get your guitar out of the case while this record's still playing. We won't be able to make noise while Wayne's talking," Jimmy said then turned to the sitting man. "You doing okay today, Wayne?"

"I'm doing great, Jimmy. Who's your helper, here?"

"This young man's gonna sing on the show today." He scratched his head. "What did you say your name is, sonny?"

"Tommy, Tommy Kizziah."

Wayne stuck out his hand. "Nice to meet you, Tom. Now you'd better hurry, I'm only going to play one more record after this one then y'all are on the air."

He placed the case on the floor, flipped the latches and got out his old guitar. "Where do you want me to sit?"

"Right there." Jimmy pointed to the empty chair. "I'll sit where Wayne is, so I can run the soundboard."

So that's what they called that thing with all the knobs. A

soundboard. "Man, I'd never be able to work that thing. How do you remember what to do?"

"Well, to tell the truth, I don't know much about it. I just simply turn on what I need to do my show and someone had to show me how to do that." He chuckled. "So ya see, I'm no smarter about this thing than you are."

Jimmy reached for his guitar, which was sitting in the corner. "Now, when he starts the next record, we'd better make sure We're in tune with each other. We only have a couple more minutes before show time."

"Shhhhh."

Tommy watched Wayne pull the microphone closer to his mouth. He already had another record placed on the second turntable ready to go.

"That was a good one, wasn't it folks? Now, right after this next song, you're in for a real treat. It's almost time for the Jimmy Rogers show. Fifteen minutes of live music from Mr. Jimmy Rogers himself, so go get the rest of the family and gather up around the radio." He pushed the turntable to get it started and the last song began.

Wayne got out of his chair. "Okay, Jim, have a seat, I'll introduce you then you know what to do."

Jimmy took his place. "Yep, sure do," He turned his attention to Tommy. "Now, lets get tuned."

He strummed his guitar, and so did Jimmy. Amazed that they only had to make a few minor adjustments to the strings. It was surprising to him that he wasn't more nervous than he was. Shoot, there was nothing to doing a radio show. If you couldn't see who you were singin' for, why be scared? Right? Who was he tryin' to fool. His heart's poundin' was lettin' him know the truth.

Wayne leaned over Jimmy and fiddled with a couple of things on the console.

"Ready, sonny?" Jimmy asked.

He tried to calm the butterflies in his stomach. "I reckon."

Even though he didn't know what Mr. Rogers had planned for the show, he sat up straight in the chair and poised himself to play.

"Here we go." Wayne cleared his throat. "Hope you enjoyed that one folks. Now for your special daily treat. I'm proud to introduce the Blue Yodeler, Mr. Jimmy Rogers. Jimmy?"

"Oh, thank ya, Wayne, thank ya. I'm glad to be here. I'd like to invite all you folks down to the theater tonight for my show. It starts at eight o'clock and I'd like to see y'all there.

"I want to let you know, that in just a little bit, here on the radio show, I'm gonna have a special guest sing a song for ya, but right now, I'm gonna sing one and it goes like this," He plucked the strings on his guitar and started to sing. "All around the water tank..."

Tommy sat with his mouth open. He couldn't help it. Jimmy Rogers was singin' right there in front of him. In the flesh, and they were the only two in the room. His maw and God were surely watchin' over him. Goose bumps rose on his body and he shivered. The pure sound of the man's voice vibrated every inch of him. Life couldn't get any better than this. No better at all.

When Jimmy finished, Tommy caught himself talkin' without meanin' to. "That was great! Wow!" He felt like an idiot when Jimmy frowned and put a finger to his lips to shush him. What a dummy. They were on the air. His first chance to impress Jimmy Rogers and he blew it. He just knew he'd never be on the show again. Not after that.

"Why, thank ya, Sonny."

What? He answered him?

"Folks, I want to introduce you to my pal, here. This young man can really sing, and I'm gonna get him to sing for you now. Sonny, you ready?"

Something in his mind clicked and the fourteen year old boy stepped aside to let the professional musician takeover. "Ready, Jimmy, if you don't mind me singin' one of your songs."

"That's fine, just fine. Which one are you gonna do, Sonny?"

"How about Sleep Baby Sleep."

"All righty. Folks here's...here's...Sonny, to sing Sleep Baby Sleep." Jimmy pushed the microphone toward Tommy.

Guitar in perfect tune, Tommy kicked off the song and was pleased when Jimmy joined in with his instrument. Making sure he was singing right into the mic, he began. A smile almost as broad as the room, lifted the corners of Mr. Rogers' mouth. He liked it! He really liked it.

When the song came to a certain part, Jimmy began to harmonize with him. He would never be able to describe the pride and happiness he felt at that moment. He was on top of the world. He finished singing, and Jimmy pulled the microphone back.

"That was real good, Sonny. I hope everybody out there who sings my songs sings them that good. Folks you can look for Sonny to be on the show again tomorrow, so be sure and tune in."

Tomorrow? Hells bells, he was gonna be on again tomorrow! Tommy sat back in his chair and waited quietly while Jimmy finished the remaining time with a couple more songs. Fifteen minutes wasn't very long at all and he didn't want it to end but knew when Wayne stepped back into the room, it was over.

While Jimmy was still talking into the mic, he stood and Wayne took a seat. "Thank you, folks, very much and now I'm gonna turn things back over to Wayne."

Wayne pulled the microphone to his mouth. "Ah, thank ya, Jimmy. What a treat, right folks? Now, here's a good record for you out there in radio land." He spun the record, put the needle in its place and the music started.

It was safe to talk now. "Mr. Rogers, that was fun. Thank you for letting me on."

"You bet ya. I'm sorry I couldn't remember your name. That's why I called you Sonny."

"That's okay, I kinda like that name."

"Then tomorrow when you come on, we'll leave your name

Sonny. Sonny Rogers, how bout that?"

Tommy swallowed hard and just knew his eye balls were about twice as big as normal. He couldn't believe this all was happening so fast. "Sonny Rogers would be fine with me, sir."

Jimmy laughed. "Okay, Sonny, I'll see you tomorrow."

He watched the older man walk away. Tomorrow, tomorrow! What was he going to do for the rest of the day and tonight? He had no clothes, no food and no place to stay. If he was going to be here all night he knew he'd better call Jack. His Paw was already gonna be mad, there was no need to make it worse by not callin' in.

Quickly he ran to catch up with Mr. Rogers. "Jimmy? Sir?"

"Yeah, Sonny, what is it?

"Is there a phone I can use? I need to call my brother in El Reno and tell him I ain't gonna get home today."

"El Reno. You live in El Reno?"

"Yes, Sir."

"How'd you get to the City?"

"I hitched a ride with an old man. He brought me straight to the station."

"What does your paw think about you comin' here?"

He glanced down at his feet. "To tell the truth, he don't know," he answered, then met the man's gaze once again. He could almost see wheels turning in Jimmy's head. He hoped this didn't ruin things for him. Maybe Jimmy was going to change his mind about having him on the show and make him go home.

A frown creased Jimmy's brow. "I see."

He'd seen that look on his paw's face before. At this point, it didn't look good. The longer Mr. Rogers thought about it the more he thought. Yep, that's it. I'm a goner! May as well get my thumb warmed up. "I'll just get my guitar, Sir."

"Yeah, you do that." His furrowed brow lifted. "I think I know of a place you can stay tonight. Are those overalls the only clothes you've got with you?"

This couldn't be true. He was gonna let him stay? "Yes, Sir."

"Do you have any money?"

"Ten dollars."

"That's quite a lot of cash. It should last you for a few days. Now, go get your guitar. I'm going to make a phone call, then we'll make yours."

He wanted to jump up and down, but he tried to keep his cool. Showing childishness right now wasn't the right thing to do. Quietly he stepped into the small broadcasting room and gathered his guitar, giving a silent wave to Wayne.

As he walked back into the hallway, he wondered if he was going to get to spend the night with Mr. Rogers. No, that was dreaming a little too much. Just as he approached the desk in the lobby, Jimmy placed the phone receiver in its cradle.

"You're all set with a place to stay, Sonny. That is, of course, if your paw says it's okay. So, we'd better give him a call."

"Well, we don't have a phone at our house." He dug a piece of paper out of his pocket. "This is the number to Tillman's Hardware where my brother works. I'm supposed to call there."

"Then we'll just do that." He took the paper from Tommy and handed it to the lady behind the desk. "Will you get this number for me, please?"

"Right away, Jimmy."

"Sonny, I have a couple of friends that are barbers. You'll be staying with them. They'll give you a good haircut, a bath and I'll bring you some clothes."

"Here you go, Sonny, it's ringing," the young woman interrupted.

Hells bells, was everyone gonna call him Sonny? "Thank ya." He couldn't bring himself to look her in the eye as he took the receiver. She was too pretty and he was cockeyed.

"Hello, Mr. Tillman?"

"Yes."

"This is Tom Kizziah. Is my brother Jack there? I need to talk to him."

"Sure, sure, Tom, I'll get him."

The wait seemed like it lasted for hours, but he knew it was really only seconds.

"Hello."

He recognized Jack's voice right away. "Jack, it's Tom."

"Tom, hey, I thought I heard you on Jimmy Rogers" radio show a while ago, but it was somebody named Sonny, but he sounded just like you."

"I am Sonny."

"What?"

"I was on the show."

"You were? That was you?"

"Yep, and he wants me to be on tomorrow, too."

"No kiddin'? You scoundrel. I thought Paw would kill you for goin' to the City, but I think you probably just saved your own ass!

"Oh, sorry Mr. Tillman, but that was my brother on the radio with Jimmy Rogers, and he's gonna be on again tomorrow. I'm just excited, that's all."

He heard Jack's second conversation and laughed. "Jack, I'm gonna stay the night here."

Jimmy's voice caught his attention.

"Maybe a few days, Sonny. Let's see what happens after tomorrow."

"Or maybe a few days, Jack. Will you tell Paw for me? Please?"

"Sure, I'll tell him as soon as he gets home. Where you gonna sleep?"

"Jimmy's got that all fixed up. I'll be okay."

"Man, the real Jimmy Rogers. You lucky dog. Did he talk to you?

"Well, of course he did. He's standin' right here."

Jimmy reached for the receiver. "Hi, Jack, This is Jimmy Rogers. I'm gonna take care of your brother, don't you worry about that. Just tell your paw to call the station if he has any questions or wants Sonny to come home. Okay, here's your brother back."

Tom took the receiver back but didn't hear anything on the other end. "Jack, you there?" Nothing. "Jack?!"

"Yeah, TH, I'm here. Just can't believe I just talked to him, that's all."

"Well, I gotta go, but you give Paw the message."

"Sure, I will. Bye."

The receiver fit perfectly on the wall hook when he replaced it. "Okay, Mr. Rogers, I'm ready."

* * *

Tommy stepped out of the car and looked at the neat little white house. Black shutters framed the windows and flowers lined the sidewalk leading to the porch. He heard Jimmy's door shut and turned to face him. "Is this where the barbers live?"

"Yep. This is where you'll be staying, Sonny. They have an extra bedroom just for you."

"I ain't never had my own bedroom. I've always had to sleep with my brothers."

A woman's voice startled him, and he flinched when he turned to meet her gaze.

"Well, not here young man. You'll have your very own bed, all by yourself."

The lady was young and beautiful. Tom was speechless and had to force his mouth shut so she wouldn't think he was a total idiot.

Jimmy stepped forward. "Sonny, this is Maxine, she's one of the barbers I told you about."

"A-a lady barber?" Well, that statement sounded dumb.

"Two of them, Sonny, two of them."

Maxine put her arm around his shoulders and gave him a hug. "It's okay," she said, "We won't hurt you."

Her smile was warm but the hug threw him off guard. He'd never been around many beautiful women and her closeness stirred something inside him. She smelled sweet, and clean.

"No, no ma'am, I know you won't hurt me. I'm not feared. I was just expectin' a couple of guys, that's all."

She took his guitar from him and led the way into the house. "Isn't it funny how everyone thinks barbers should be men. Why, me and Lilly have had our own little barber shop almost two years now. We do a good business, too."

He watched her behind swish back and forth as she took the few steps up to the door. "Yes, ma'am, I'm sure you do."

Jimmy nudged him with his elbow and brought him out of his adolescent stupor. He felt silly and disrespectful looking at Maxine's bottom like that, but he couldn't help it. He could see that Jimmy was admiring it, too. He smiled and so did the older man. Suddenly he felt like he was growing up.

"Sonny, you're room's right here." Maxine put his guitar on the floor in front of the small bed. "And the bathroom's just down the hall. We'll run you a bath in a little bit and get some of that dirt off of you."

He hoped she didn't think she was gonna give him a bath. "Yes, ma'am, thank you."

"Jimmy, you're going to bring him some clothes, right?"

"Actually, they're in the car. We stopped by and picked them up on the way over. I'll get them."

Jimmy left the small room and Tommy's heart pounded in his chest when Maxine reached for him and ran her fingers through his hair. Her touch was warm and he liked it. He really liked it.

"You have quite the head of hair there, Sonny. So wavy and black, it's very nice. A good haircut is all you need. After Lilly gets home and you get your bath, we'll go to the shop and give you one." She took his chin between her thumb and fingers and studied his face, moving his head from side to side. "You're a very handsome young man. Very handsome. What happened to your eye?"

His eye. He'd almost forgotten about it. He moved away from her grasp and looked away. "I was born like this. Never have been able to see good outta that eye. My maw always said I need specks."

"Well, well, well, we'll just have to see if we can't do something about that."

"Something about what?" Jimmy asked, returning with the bag of clothes.

"Jimmy, this boy needs glasses and I just happen to cut the hair of a good eye doctor."

"I cain't afford no glasses, ma'am."

She laughed. "Sonny, you won't have to pay for them."

"Let me see that eye, Sonny." Jimmy said.

He glanced up at Mr. Rogers and looked him square in the eyes with his good one.

"Hmmmm. Well, if Maxine can get you in to see the doc. I'll pay for you some glasses for being on the show the next few days. How's that sound?"

Was this truly happening? Was he gonna get some specks and really be able to see? "Thank you, Jimmy, that sounds great!" The smile that crossed his face felt good. These folks really cared about him and they didn't even know him. How about that!

The screen door slammed shut and a woman yelled out. "Max, I'm home with the groceries."

Maxine smiled. "That's your other roommate, Sonny. Let's go help her bring in the grub."

"I have to go," Jimmy informed them. "I've got to get ready for the show at the theater. You girls gonna bring Sonny down there tonight?"

"I don't think so," Maxine ruffled Tom's hair. "We're going to get him all fixed up. He'll look like a different young man next time you see him. We'll bring him tomorrow night."

"Okay, I'll be here to pick him up for the radio show at noon tomorrow."

"He'll be ready."

Tommy helped the ladies get their bags out of the car and followed them inside. Lilly was pretty, but not quite as much of a looker as Max. He helped Lilly put away the groceries and had never seen some of the things they had in their cabinets. Hell's bells, they even had store bought cookies they kept in a big glass jar. His folks could never afford this kind of food.

"Okay, Sonny, I've drawn your bath," Max said. "You ready?"

A good hot bath did sound good. He was tired as all get out. "Yes, ma'am, I believe so."

Lots of things had happened in his life in just one day. Hitchin' a ride for the first time. Singin' on a radio show with the real live Jimmy Rogers. Getting to stay with two pretty women and havin' his own room with his very own bed. And maybe tomorrow he would get some glasses. Man oh man...life was good.

"I've laid your clean clothes out on the bed. You go on into the bathroom and get in the tub. Your clean unders are in there."

He went into the bathroom, took off his clothes and placed them in a heap on the floor. After relieving himself he stepped into the deep tub full of water, leaned against the back and totally relaxed into the warmth. He had just closed his eyes when he heard the door open. Looking up he saw Max and Lilly standing in the doorway, both wearing wide grins.

He quickly sat up and covered his privates. "What are you ladies doin?"

They stepped inside and as Lilly closed the door behind them, Max said, "We're going to help you get every speck of dirt off."

His heart jumped in his chest as they knelt beside the tub. What were they gonna do? He was fourteen; he could give himself a bath. "I-I can do it. You ladies don't need to help."

Max took the washcloth and the bar of soap. Lilly gently pushed on his chest and said. "Now, you just lay back and relax. This won't hurt a bit."

CHAPTER 6

January 1930

Jimmy Rogers and another man walked into the kitchen at Max and Lilly's house. Tommy stood to greet them.

Jimmy introduced the man. "Sonny, this is Doc Foxhorn. He's the one I was telling you about."

Mr. Foxhorn nodded his hello. "Mr. Rogers here thinks you would be good on our medicine show. What do you think?"

"I agree, sir. I can do a lot of things for you besides sing. I'm good and strong. And my paw's a musician, too. He could probably help out."

"Is he now. Well, we'll see if we can find a place for him, too, if you want."

He did want it. He missed his paw and with the money he'd saved over the last few months, he could send for him and they could both be on the Foxhorn's show. Surely now that his eye was getting better his paw wouldn't be embarrassed.

"I'd like that very much."

Half daydreaming while Mr. Foxhorn and Jimmy talked further; he gazed in the direction of El Reno. All his brothers were there and he missed them, too, but he couldn't afford to send for them. Jimmy's voice grabbed his attention.

"Sonny, Mr. Foxhorn's going to leave now."

"Oh, sorry. I was thinking about my paw."

"If you miss him that much, we'll definitely find a place for him on the show. Don't you worry."

"Thank you, Mr. Foxhorn, for everything."

"You're welcome young Sonny Rogers. I'll be seeing you soon."

"Yes, sir." The man shook his hand and left.

Jimmy pulled a chair out from the table. "Sonny, let's sit down."

He followed Jimmy's lead. "Is something wrong?"

"No, I just want to talk to you, that's all. Sonny, I've wanted to tell you this for some time now. You know I've got a daughter, right?"

"Yes, sir."

"Well, you're like the son I never had. I wish you could go with me, but I think you need to be with your family."

He swallowed hard to choke down the lump in his throat. He'd never seen Jimmy so emotional, but he could swear there were tears in the man's eyes.

"You've come a long way in the last few weeks, and I've grown to love you, "

What was he supposed to say? "We-well, I love you, too."

"Sonny, I want you to do something for me."

"Anything, Jimmy, you name it."

"I want you to learn every new song you can. I've never heard anyone who could sing as good as you. You really have a talent, boy."

Never had he been so swollen with pride as he was that moment. Hells bells, this was Jimmy Rogers telling him this. Man oh man. "Thank ya, Jimmy. I'll do my best."

"I know you will. You go on that show with the Foxhorns and learn everything you can. He's going to take your daddy, too, for sure."

"Good, I have enough money saved up that I can send him a train ticket."

"Don't you worry about getting him a ticket, Doc's going

to take care of that."

Wow, he was going to get to keep his money after all. Why were all of these people being so nice? He wasn't sure, but was thankful for it and would be sure to thank God in his prayers tonight.

* * *

Tommy leaned out of the passenger side window of the car his paw was driving, and looked toward the porch of the little white house. He was going to miss Max, Lilly and Jimmy. The last sixteen weeks of his life had changed him forever.

He'd had his fifteenth birthday, made a name in music, even if it wasn't his real one, he had glasses, his eye looked normal and he could see for the first time in his life. He'd never known how beautiful everything was. And it was all because of the three people standing on that porch.

Max blew him a kiss. "Keep in touch, Sonny."

He didn't blush when he thought of all the things Max and Lilly had taught him. The embarrassment of the boy he was when he met them flew out the window long ago. They sure enough made a man out of him and he liked it. "I will Max. And thank y'all for everything."

"We love you, Sonny." Lilly wiped a tear from her eye.

"Don't cry. I'll come visit."

His Paw turned the key and the engine roared to life. "We're goin' now, Son."

He waved as the car pulled away from the curb. "Bye. Thanks again. I love y'all, too."

"They were mighty good to you. Why, you got enough new clothes in that suitcase to last you for years, if you don't grow out of 'em," Lon said.

"Yes, sir, they were. I'm gonna miss 'em."

"I know, but it's time for Mr. Rogers to leave the City and move on. He's a mighty good man to have gotten us a place on the Foxhorn's show. Sonny Rogers is a well known name in these parts now, and you'll be able to pull a lot of people and make some money. With this depression goin' on, money's hard to come by."

It was going to be a long road to South Carolina to practice and get the show together. They'd bring the show back to Texas as soon as everyone was ready with their parts, and the trucks and tents were ready.

It had been a long time since he'd seen his grandma Lyd and he hoped they'd get a chance to stop and see her while they were in the state. His uncles were good workers and were supporting her as best they could.

The depression had everyone scared, but his family had always been poor so it was something he was used to. His paw didn't know Jimmy had paid him for doing the radio show all those weeks.

He'd decided not to tell him either. Not trying to be selfish or anything, but he wanted to save the money and buy himself a car. He would share what he made on the medicine show with his family. That wasn't being selfish, was it? Maybe he'd share his money with his grandma. His paw's voice drew him from his thoughts.

"And, T.H. I'm gonna call you Sonny, and I've decided to use the name Rogers, too. I think it will help us all the way around. From now on, I'll be Lon Rogers and you'll be Sonny. Doc said since I'm gonna play the banjo on the show, he's gonna call me Banjo Lon. Okay?"

"I've been Sonny Rogers for almost four months now, it won't make any difference to me. I'm already used to it. I think Banjo Lon fits you just fine, Paw."

"Good, then that's what we'll do."

* * *

August 1931

"Do you, Lon, take this woman Myrtle Marie Gummalt to be your lawful wedded wife, to have and to hold until death do you part?"

Lon Smiled. "I do."

"And do you, Myrtle Gummalt, take this man Elick Alonzo Rogers to be your lawful wedded husband, to have and to hold until death do you part?"

"I do, sir."

Myrt's accent was strong as she spoke in broken English, even with just those three words. Tommy liked the German girl his Father met and chose to marry.

He thought of her as a girl because she was only two years older than he was. Did she even know her new husband was thirty years older then she was? He didn't think so.

His paw had asked him to call him Lon so people would think they were brothers instead of father and son. Lon had even told her that Bill, Jack and Red were his brothers. But that was his paw's business, not his. As long as Myrtle loved Lon, that's all that counted.

She was from Brenham, Texas and had been coming to the shows in the area for quite some time. He knew she'd caught his paw's eye the first time he saw her, but it never crossed his mind that his paw would marry the young woman.

He listened as Reverend Badenhead finished the ceremony.

"Mr. Rogers, you may kiss the bride."

Why wasn't the Reverend using his paw's real last name? Oh, well, show stuff he guessed. It probably didn't matter. At least they knew their real name was Kizziah.

His haw kissed Myrtle, and Tommy smiled when the crowd of over two hundred, including Myrt's parents, erupted in applause. It was the first wedding on the medicine show, and the people liked it. Now the music would start and the selling begin.

"Go on, Sonny, y'all play something," Myrt said and started to leave the stage, but Lon asked her to stay beside him for at least one number.

Guitar in hand, he took his place on the front of the small

stage. "I'm ready." He had taken over being the front person on the show this year at his paw's request. He liked it and was good at it, too.

As soon as the rest of the players were ready, he got started. "Howdy folks, how'd you like that weddin' here in Buffalo, Texas?"

Claps once again cracked the air. "Good, good. It was a mighty fine weddin' indeed, and I got me a new friend. She's a short little thing, but she's a good cook." He patted the top of Myrt's head and laughter filtered through the crowd. He liked to tease her about being so small and she went right along with the joke. "She can't pluck the strings off a banjo but Billy can and this is one of my new friend's favorite tunes. Myrt, wha-da-ya-say we start with a little Cripple Creek?"

Her eyes sparkled and she nodded, then Billy began to plunk out the tune, the rest of the musicians joined in. The people bounced and kept time to the music. Watching the crowd and seeing the joy on their faces was what Tommy loved most about entertaining. If he could touch folks' hearts and make their life better in any way, that was good enough for him. Of course, the money was important, too.

He glanced over at his shiny new car. Well it wasn't really new, but it was new to him, and he was thankful for his good fortune. He didn't have anything else, but he had a nice car he could depend on to get him around.

The depression hit everyone hard. He had done without many times over the last couple of years, but was determined to save the money for a car, and he'd done it. However, he was saddened that some of the folks were devastated by their losses. That's why he was glad the show brought so much fun to so many.

"Well, now, that was really good, wasn't it Myrt?" She acknowledged his question, kissed her new husband and took her leave. Tommy again focused his attention to the audience.

"Good enough to have the folks dancin' where they stand.

I'll bet a lot of you are dancin' because you've tried our tonic. This tonic will really help what ails ya. It'll make those aches and pains disappear."

He went on with the rest of the sales speech, knowing that the tonic was made up of a little medicine and a lot of whiskey. But, it did seem to really help the folks who believed in it, and he wasn't a doctor, so who was he to say it was all in their minds.

He pointed at Doc Foxhorn, behind the sales table. Doc owned the show and was the one who made up the tonic. "Visit that feller right there, give him your fifty cents and he'll get you feelin' better in no time." He glanced back at the band. "Let's play boys." Already knowing what song to kick off, the band played and the show was on once again.

The celebration went well into the night and the next morning everyone slept in. The smell of bacon drifting across the air, along with the aroma of fresh baked, homemade biscuits, roused Tommy from sleep. He didn't know how Myrt did it. She could cook almost anything on the open fire outside the ragged tents of their camp area.

The sound of the little woman's voice reached his ears through the tent.

"Sonny, get up, it's time to get started around here."

She had truly taken over at being the mother figure of the show troop. It almost felt like they were a family again. Even though Jack, Bill and Red had gone their own ways, and he was the only one of the brothers left, when he was with a show, everyone was like family.

He took a place by the fire and she sat a plate of bacon with biscuits and gravy in front of him.

His paw sat down beside him and cleared his throat. "Well, Sonny, me and Myrtle have decided not to go on no more medicine shows. We're gonna settle down. I'm getting older and she wants to have a family, so I guess we're going to try to have a baby."

A Baby? He couldn't believe his ears. The man was goin' on fifty years old. Hells bells, Ike was almost thirty. Why, he himself was nearly seventeen. "A baby, Paw? I mean, Lon." That slipped out from shock, he guessed.

Lon nodded. "She and I've been talkin' about this for the last couple of months. Once we decided to marry, we knew we wanted to make some changes in our lifestyle. We just didn't want to tell ya till after the weddin'. We were afraid it would ruin the party for you and the rest of the folks last night if everyone knew."

"I understand. It's okay, I've been thinking about moving on myself." This was perfect. He'd wanted to go back to South Carolina with Doc, and continue to work with the Foxhorns. The Foxhorn family treated him like he belonged, and he felt right at home. He didn't know why his breathing wasn't as good there, but he still wanted to go back.

"Me and Fred have been talkin' about goin' back to Carolina. I like it there and he misses his family."

"Well...Myrt, if you're worried about the folks around here knowin' too much, maybe we should go to Carolina, too." Lon sipped his coffee. "You think about it, Hon, and let me know what you want to do."

This young woman had a control over his father that he'd never seen before. Usually, his paw was the one who called all the shots, but Myrt had it in the bag. She was some kind of woman. Strong, smart and though she'd gained a little weight, pretty, too, but not as pretty as one girl he knew.

He took another bite of biscuit and let his thoughts wander back to South Carolina. Little did he know that when Doc hired him, and they went to Carolina to put the show together, the man had a beautiful daughter. When he met her he thought she was the prettiest girl in the world. Maggie Foxhorn. And now he was gonna go back there to see her again.

Maggie had been on his mind almost every waking moment since he'd left her. Her pretty face wafted across his thoughts and butterflies flitted in his stomach.

Although, he hadn't told anyone of his love for her, one day he planned to marry her. He hoped she'd say yes, but he knew he had to have something to offer her first. Her family had been more fortunate than his, and she was used to a different lifestyle. He prayed he could live up to the challenge.

December 1931,

"How ya feelin' Myrt?"

"Tired, Lon, but okay. How's the baby?"

"He's fine. Maw's takin' good care of him."

"I'm glad she could come to be with us. You were right. I do love her."

"I wrote your folks a letter tellin' them the baby came and that we named him Allen."

She looked down. "Now they're gonna know I was pregnant when we got married."

Lon put his finger under her chin and forced her to look at him. "It doesn't matter, Myrt. We care for each other, that's all that counts. Now you stop frettin' about that, ya hear? They're gonna love you either way."

The rap of knuckles sounded against the wooden door in the small room. Lon kissed his wife and smiled. "It's probably Maw bringin' Allen to ya. Come in."

Tommy entered the room holding a tiny bundle. "Guess who's here?" He approached the bed where Myrt lay. "It's my baby br—nephew." Smiling, he placed the newborn beside its mother. He almost let the cat out of the bag. Thank God he'd stopped himself. "He sure is handsome, y'all."

A tear rolled down the young mother's cheek as she took in the sight of her first child. "He sure is."

"What did you decide to name the little feller?"

"Allen. Allen Rogers," replied Myrt.

"And a fine name that is." Tommy turned toward his father and offered a handshake. "Congratulations."

Lon stood and grasped his son's hand. "Thank ya, Sonny. How ya been?"

"Good. Been pretty boring at the Foxhorn's fillin' station over the winter and now we're gettin' busier. I've been workin' between there and their motel. We'll start getting ready for the show in a few weeks."

"How's Doc and his family?"

"Fine."

Lon smiled. "And how's that pretty little Maggie doin?"

Tommy's breath caught in his chest at the mention of her name. In the last few months, everyone could see how he felt about her. He couldn't hide it any more. He grinned and answered, "She's doin' great."

"Any wedding bells comin' up?"

"Naw, not yet." Money was the only thing stopping him from asking for her hand, but right now, it just wasn't possible. "Maybe someday."

Silver haired Lyd walked into the room holding a cup. Tommy had been glad to see his grandmother, but was surprised to learn she had remarried a man named Mr. Jackson. The full blood Cherokee woman was still beautiful, and sure spry for her age. He didn't really know how old she was, but she had to be older than two trees.

"Got that baby to suckin' yet, Myrt?" the older woman asked.

"No, ma'am, I've just been looking at him."

Lyd placed the cup on the table beside the bed. "Well, you set up a little bit. I brought ya some broth." She directed her attention to her son and grandson. "You boys get outta here so Myrt can learn how to give this youngun' some milk. They both need nourishment after what they've been through."

"Yes'm," Lon replied and followed Tommy out of the room.

* * *

Tommy approached the tiny grave. It had been a couple of weeks before Christmas when Allen was born. Now in mid January of nineteen thirty-two, the baby had passed on, and he was another year older. Sometimes he didn't understand life.

His heart went out to his stepmother. She had nearly lost her mind with grief because of her loss. The doctor didn't know what caused the baby to stop breathing in its sleep, but said it happened from time to time and there was nothing Myrt could have done. Now, she knelt by her little one's graveside and sobbed.

Lost for words, Tommy took his Paw's place by her side while Lon took his leave to offer thanks to the folks who had attended the services. He searched the crowd for Maggie. When their gaze met he was comforted by the reassuring smile in her eyes. Nodding his thanks for her being there, he turned his attention back to Myrtle.

The hours after the funeral service turned into days and the days into weeks. Tommy had seen Myrt and Lon only a few times in between, they lived in Spartanburg and he'd moved to Society Hill. It was a few hours drive from one place to the other. However, he loved living in Society Hill because he got to see Maggie so much.

It was coming into spring now, and she was more radiant than ever. Her smile matched the beauty of the flowers that were beginning to bloom. But soon he'd have to leave her behind to play on the show. He hoped she'd be waiting for him when he got back.

From behind the cluttered desk, through the window of the filling station where he worked, he watched her walk across the parking lot of the motel and come toward him. His loins stirred when her hips swished from side to side. She didn't fool him. She knew exactly what she did to him. She tortured him, but he liked that kind of torture, even though they had never made love, it didn't stop him from wanting her. Maybe it made him want her more.

The bell hanging on the door sounded when she entered. "Hi there, handsome."

"Howdy. How's my favorite girl?"

"Fine, now that I've seen you."

It was all he could do to keep from pulling her to him and kissing her. Nightfall would come in a few hours. That wouldn't be soon enough for him, but it would have to do, and he'd forced himself to wait until then to hold her in his arms and taste her sweet lips.

She smiled and his heart melted into his shoes. How did she do that to him? There was an electrified silence in the room and sparks flew until the service bell rang outside alerting him there was a customer. He hated to take his gaze from hers. "I gotta go to work, pretty girl."

He shifted his eyes toward the car that had pulled in. "Well, hells bells, there's my Paw and Myrt. They've made a pretty long drive; I hope everything's okay. I'll be right back. Don't go away."

"Oh, I won't."

After pulling the door open, he stepped outside. "What brings you two to our little town of Society Hill?" Myrt's passenger window was open. He bent down and placed his elbows on the metal car door frame. Funny, Myrt was smiling and so were her eyes. In the few times he'd seen them since Allen's death, this was the first she looked happy.

Lon sat forward. "Good news, Sonny. Myrt's with child again. Why, with Allen passin' and everything, we're really happy about it. Looks like the new baby'll be here in November."

He leaned in and gave his stepmother a hug. "That's great news. And I'll be back from doin' the show by then, too, so maybe I can come see y'all. Maybe at Thanksgivin'." He looked at Myrtle. "You gonna name it after me? If it's a boy, that is."

"Not on your life," she answered. "You're too ornery.

We're gonna name him after your granddaddy James. We're not sure about a name for a girl."

Her German accent was strong and cheerful. His heart felt hope went out to the woman sitting in front of him, that the baby would live to be a ripe old age. "Good luck to you, Myrt. Everything will be all right this time." He kissed her cheek. "How long ya stayin' in town?"

"Oh, a couple of days," Lon answered. We just decided to make the trip over here to give you the news, and to see everyone. We're gonna get a room at the motel. Thought we might pick and grin a little bit tonight."

"Sounds like fun to me. Y'all need gas?"

"May as well fill it up now instead of when we get ready to leave."

"Okay," Tommy started the pump, then returned to the window.

"When are y'all gonna go out on the road for the show?" his paw asked.

"Not sure. Should start practice soon, though." The sound of Maggie's voice startled him and he stood straight up, bumping his head on the top of the car door. "Hells bells." Her laughter at his reaction warmed his heart.

"That's what I came to tell ya."

"What?"

"When you're leaving. I'm supposed to watch the station because Dad wants you to come practice. He said y'all are starting out next week."

Tommy's mouth lifted at the corners. He couldn't wait to get back to playing again, but leaving her behind for the season was another thing. He turned his attention back to his father. "I guess that answers the question, then."

"Guess so. Well, we'll leave y'all to your business. Maggie, it's good to see ya again. We'll be seein' you later."

Tommy put his arm around Maggie's shoulder and watched the couple's car move away to make the short trip to the motel across the street. Myrt waved from the window. He was happy for them. But mostly he was glad to have Maggie by his side. "Hey, what do you think about givin' me a little kiss?" Her eyes sparkled when she met his gaze.

"Out here in plain sight? Are you crazy? My Dad would have your hide." A mischievous grin crossed her face. "Let's go inside and you'll see what kind of a kiss I can give you."

CHAPTER 7

Fall 1942

Tommy pulled the car over to a rest stop. All those years living in South Carolina he wondered why at times he'd wheeze and cough. He worried he might have TB, but that wasn't it at all. He had asthma. At least that's what the Army doctors said. He shook his head. Damn, he didn't get to serve his full four years in the service. The disease wouldn't allow it. He looked down at the discharge papers on the car seat. Boot camp was barely over and he was already a civilian again.

War was upon the great United States, and he wouldn't be able to fight beside the friends and comrades he'd gotten to know over the last few months. How many of them would die in combat? He didn't really want to know.

He picked up the documents, glanced through them, then put them back in their resting place. Why did he even look at them? He couldn't read. Unlike playing the guitar, reading was something he couldn't teach himself. Oh, well, he knew what they said. He was out of the Army for good, and he was only twenty-seven years old.

Lying back in the seat, he closed his eyes. The drive from Sumter, South Carolina, to Lubbock, Texas, was a long one, and there were a couple of stops he wanted to make on the way.

He was half way there, but right now he just wanted to rest

for a while. Lawton, Oklahoma, was still about five hours away and he didn't want to be completely beat when he was reunited with his baby sister, Mary. She didn't know he was coming and he couldn't wait to surprise her. He hadn't seen her since she was a girl. Now, she was all grown up and had a daughter of her own.

How quickly time passed. His mind traced back over the past ten years and what they had brought.

He smiled. 1932. Myrt had little James in October. It was a few weeks early, but the boy was fine. Then in '33' she and his Paw decided to move to Rockwood to be close to his grandma Lyd. His paw was making tonic of his own and sell-ing it to the locals.

Sadness came in the spring of '33', when he learned of the death of his friend and mentor, Jimmy Rogers. How could he have not kept in touch with the man who meant so much to him? Well, Jimmy knew how he felt about him and that's all that mattered.

In '34' they sent word that Myrt had had twins, a boy and a girl. Elick Jr. and Ella. He remembered thinking, hells bells, two at a time, what a great thing. It was that year he'd gotten his own little place in Society Hill, South Carolina. It wasn't much, two rooms, but it was better than living in a motel room and it was his.

Jack married in '34', and in '35' his wife had their first baby, a boy, Jack Jr. Mary's daughter, Mary Lou, was also born in '35'. Then in '36', Jack's wife had a little girl they named Janie, after his Maw. He was proud of his big brother for that; and pleased they had kept in contact, even if they only talked once a year or so.

Myrt had another baby girl in the early part of '37' and named her Ivy. She was havin' babies right and left, but that's what she wanted, a big family.

Then the bad news came. He received a telegram inform-ing him of his father's death in December of '37'. Lon and

Myrt had moved to DeQueen, Arkansas, from Rockwood. His condolences went out in the form of a letter that Maggie helped him write. He didn't have the money to go to the funeral. Even though he hadn't seen the man in a few years, somehow he missed him, but not nearly as much as he still missed his maw.

In the winters of those years, he continued to work for the Foxhorns and play for a few dances. In summers he played on the medicine show. It wasn't great money, but it kept the bills paid. The Foxhorns told him he wouldn't be able to make a living doing anything because he didn't have an education, so he'd have to rely on his music.

And Maggie . . . Maggie grew into a beautiful, sophisticated young lady. Her folks sent her to private school before their relationship blossomed, and he was close to asking her to marry him. Then in one fateful day in '38', everything changed. Her mother, who was also beautiful, made advances toward him. He had never figured out why a woman like Mrs. Foxhorn would want him, but she did, and on a few particular occasions, made no bones about it.

He sat up in the seat. With all these memories going through his mind, he'd never get any rest. He may as well be driving. He started the engine and swallowed hard at the older woman's memory.

From that day to this, it had never been the same between him and Maggie. She didn't know or understand what had torn them apart, but he couldn't break her heart, and it would, if she knew her mother wanted to have an affair with him. Worse yet, she would hate him if she found out he couldn't resist the temptation.

It hurt him to the core that he and Maggie would never marry. He had to force himself to stay out of the way when she started seeing another man, but C.L. Bailey was a good man, and Maggie deserved a good man.

He put the car in gear and merged onto the highway once again. The next few miles caught him thinking about the night in 1941 when Maggie found out he was moving to Sumter the next day. Looking back on it, it seemed like it had been longer than only a year ago, but it wasn't. His stomach churned as the memories continued.

He'd never forget the tears that glistened in the moonlight as they spilled over onto her cheek that night. His heart had thumped hard in his chest, full of love for her, but he dare not tell her. She deserved better.

Her soft hair shone in the night. She was so beautiful and he couldn't stop himself from kissing her, nor did he want to. One kiss led to another, then that led to even more. His passion for her was something he had no control over. He'd had women before, but now he knew what it was like to really make love.

She'd never been with a man in that way and he would cherish those short hours forever.

Seeing Maggie again just two days ago was harder than he'd expected, but he felt he had to tell everyone in Society Hill goodbye before he left for Texas.

She was more beautiful than ever and her baby boy looked remarkably like him. Could it be his? Yes, he knew it could have, but he never asked. C.L. didn't seem to notice the resemblance and the man loved the child and would make a great father.

He glanced into his rear view mirror and realized he wasn't paying much attention to his driving. He took a deep breath and tried to push the memories from his mind. Thoughts of his move to Sumter took over.

He had called some friends about putting together a dance band in Sumter. No one had done that in the area. They had played for a few dances here and there, but the musicians were always thrown together a couple of days before.

The music needed to be practiced and put together the right way, and you had to keep the same musicians to do that. Luckily, he got hold of his old friend Fred, and he knew some good pickers. The band they'd put together stayed busy playing until he left for the Army. Now, all to soon, that part of his life was over.

He was moving to Lubbock, Texas, where Jack and Red lived. Jack had a band and was pleased he was coming to join them.

Their grandma Lyd died while he was in boot camp. He wished he had made an effort to go see her before he went in, but it was too late now.

He checked his mirrors and pulled out to pass the car in front of him. The last road sign said Lawton was one hundred ten miles. This move to Texas would start a new life for him. He was leaving South Carolina, and its memories behind.

What would help him start over? Of course! It hit like a lightening strike. He'd use his real name instead of Sonny Rogers. Nobody in Texas knew who Sonny Rogers was, but he vowed they'd know Tommy Kizziah.

* * *

On the Fort Sill Army base in Lawton, Tommy approached the small house where he was told Mary lived. Reuben, Mary's husband, was stationed at Sill. He couldn't wait to see his sister.

Stepping up onto the little concrete porch, he noticed the door was open and he could see inside the house through the screen.

"Anybody home?"

"Be right there," said a woman's voice.

A tall young woman rounded the corner of a doorway. He knew right away it was Mary. She was a beauty with coal black hair and bright smile. A puzzled look crossed her face, then uncertainty took over as she came nearer to him.

"Oh, my God...Oh, my...Tommy? Tommy? Is that you?"

"Sure is, little sister."

Tears welled in her dark brown eyes. "I can't believe it."

She pushed open the screen door. "Get yourself in here, brother. Mary Lou! Come here, it's your Uncle Tommy."

A nine or ten year old girl came out of one of the other rooms. She also had dark hair fixed neatly with small ribbons.

"Who?"

Mary smiled. "This is my brother. He's your Uncle Tommy."

"Hi, Mary Lou. You're sure a pretty little thing."

Her grin spread from ear to ear. "You're the first uncle I've ever had."

Her mother laughed. "He's not the first uncle you've ever had. What about your uncle T.J.? You have a lot of uncles."

Tommy knelt. "That's right, and now that I'm moving back to Texas, we're all going to get together."

Mary Lou threw her arms around his neck. "Oh, when, Uncle Tommy, when?"

"Soon, I promise."

Not long into his visit, the tension left his shoulders and he was completely relaxed. He met Reuben. What a great guy. Mary brought out an old Dobro guitar to show him. The strings weren't very good on it, but it still played. She really needed a new guitar. He thought about the money he had saved. Maybe he'd just buy her one.

She fixed him a snack then took a short nap, now he was feeling much better. How good it was to be around family again. Mary was planning to fix supper soon, then she wanted to play and sing a little. Now was as good a time as any to pick her out a new guitar.

He went into the living room and found Mary sitting on the sofa. "Is there a music store in Lawton?"

"Sure, what do you need?"

"Well, ah, er, I was gonna get some new guitar picks." Guitar picks? He hoped she bought the lame excuse.

"Okay, I'll go with ya."

How was he going to pull this off? He wanted to surprise

her later tonight with his gift. "Oh, that's okay, I can find it. Don't you want to start supper?"

She stood. "Actually, Reuben said we could eat at the Officer's club tonight. This being a special occasion and all, I don't have to cook." Grabbing her handbag she said, "Mary Lou, come on, we're going into town."

What else could he do, but take the two with him? When they got to the store, he chose some picks. Mary had hold of Mary Lou's hand and was admiring the new guitars. He'd already told the store owner that he wanted to buy her a guitar, but he didn't have much money. The man led him to a dark colored Gibson F-hole guitar. It wasn't the best, but it wasn't the worst and it was in his price range.

He picked it up, tuned the strings, played a few cords and handed it to his sister. "What do you think about this one?"

"Oh, it's nice, really nice," she said as she took it from him.

She couldn't play well, but she played what she needed to be able to sing along, and she enjoyed it. Her eyes sparkled when she strummed the new Gibson.

"Sing somethin', Sis."

She handed the instrument back to him. "No, not here. I'll wait until I get home and can use my own guitar. I don't want to take a chance of something happening to that new one. It's too nice."

"So you like it?" he asked.

"Why, yes, I love it. I just don't want to break it."

He turned toward the store owner. "She needs a nice guitar. We'll take it."

"Yes, sir. I'll get the case for you."

Mary's eyes widened and she gasped. "What? No, Tommy, you can't do that!"

"I want to, little sister. It's what we came for, and it's a gift you need."

Tears streamed down her cheek. "I thought you wanted picks."

"That's what ya get for thinkin'."

* * *

Looking up at the ceiling, the evening had brought the best time Tommy had seen in a long time. He loved the smile on Mary's face when she showed off her new guitar at the Officer's club, and the shine in her eyes when she introduced him to her friends.

He enjoyed playing and singing with her. She was a joy to be around and he would never lose touch with her again. He wanted her to always be part of his life, one way or another.

The short piece of furniture where he lay wasn't very comfortable. His six foot three frame made it impossible to lie flat on the sofa, and if he did, his legs were on the arm of the thing, and his feet hung over the edge. Oh, well, he didn't care. It was just good to lie down. Fatigue caught up with him and he drifted off to sleep. Morning would come early on the Army base.

A warm hand on his shoulder gently shook him and he opened his eyes. Mary stood over him and smiled.

"You gonna sleep all day? It's seven in the morning. I've been up for hours."

"Wow, seven, it is getting late. I guess I should get up and get ready to hit the road to Texas. Hey, I have an idea. You want to go with me today. Let's have a family reunion."

She turned and went into the kitchen. "Oh, no, brother, you ain't goin' anywhere and neither am I. You're gonna rest and we're gonna visit. You have plenty of time to get to Lubbock. Besides, you surprised me with a gift, so I have a surprise for you. It'll be here later today."

* * *

The early morning sun shown through the car windshield and Tommy pulled down his visor. Mary couldn't have given him a better surprise on the day before. His baby brother had showed up early in the afternoon. Man what a sight. T.J was twenty now, stood six foot three, and was the only one of them that had a good education. He'd just gotten out of the Navy and was doing great.

Mary had some schooling, too, but no college like T.J. He was going to be a successful businessman some day. Tommy could see it happening.

He waved goodbye to his sister, her small family and T.J., then pulled his car away from the house. His trek to Lubbock would have to wait a few more days. He had another stop to make first. He was going to Brenham, Texas, to see if he could find Myrtle. Going that far South was out of his way, but he'd like to see how she was doing. If he could find her parents, maybe they could tell him where she was.

Getting such an early start, he could make the long trip in one day. He sat back in the seat, got comfortable and turned on the radio.

Music was comforting, and he drove a few hours before he stopped for gas and to eat a bite. The white clouds floating against the blue sky were a pretty contrast. The green leaves of the trees were starting to make their change to gold and red. God had done a good job on the earth when He made it, and Tommy was glad to be part of it.

Could it be he needed this trip to feed his soul? He didn't know why, but he felt free, happy and above all, his love for life was coming back. Man it was good to be alive!

He glanced toward the west. The sun was going behind the horizon, darkness was falling and he was on the outskirts of Brenham. It wasn't a very big town, so he would stop soon and inquire about Myrt's folks, Mr. and Mrs. Gummalt.

The perfect opportunity came when he saw a local cafe on the main street. Inside, the proprietor knew the Gummalts and said they had a phone. The man looked up the number for him, and let him borrow the phone. He listened as it rang once...twice.

"Hello."

The woman's German accent was evident even in this one

small word.

"Hello, Mrs. Gummalt?"

"Yes."

"Ma'am this is Tommy Kizziah, I'm looking for Myrtle."

"Who?"

"Tom...I mean Sonny, Sonny Rogers. Lon's boy." A few years before he died, Lon told Myrt the truth. That he was Lon's son, not his brother. It felt good not living with that lie anymore.

"Oh, Sonny, how are you?"

"Fine. I'm looking for Myrt. Does she live around here?"

"Yes, she does. She lives in Milk Creek. It's not far from here. Where are you?"

"At the cafe here in Brenham." He could tell she turned her face away from the phone.

"Daddy, daddy, Sonny's in Brenham and wants to see Myrtle. He's at the cafe."

A faint voice came over the earpiece that he figured to be Mr. Gummalt.

"Tell him to stay. We'll come."

"Sonny, get a cup of coffee, we'll be right there."

"I'll do 'er."

It was nice to see the older couple again. Mr. Gummalt wasn't getting around well, but he was still trying. Their hellos were brief, then they got in their separate cars and he followed their taillights through small communities and over narrow roads. After a short while, they turned onto the dirt driveway that led to a small farmhouse.

As he stepped out of his car, he saw the silhouette of a small woman peeking out from behind the curtain on the window of the front door. The curtain dropped and when the door opened, the yellow light from inside shone onto the porch.

He recognized Myrt's voice, but couldn't understand a thing she said. She was speaking in German. Finally, he heard Mrs. Gummalt say his name. Then Myrt began to speak in broken English.

"He's here?"

He stepped out of the shadows and answered her himself. "Yep, in the flesh."

"Sonny." She ran toward him, jumped up and threw her arms around his neck. "I can't believe it."

Putting his arms around her tiny waist, he returned her hug. He peered up at the house and standing in the doorway was a tall man holding a baby. Three small children stood around him. One looked as if she were stuck to the man's leg. "Is that your family?"

Myrtle released her hold on him, and he put her down. "Yes, that's my husband Gust, and those kids are your brother and sisters. They're supposed to be in bed."

A smile crossed his lips. "Well, since they're not, let's go meet the little fellers."

He followed the small woman to the house her folks were right behind. Stepping up on the porch, he offered the man his hand.

"Gust, this is Sonny Rogers, Lon's boy. He's the one I told you about."

"Nice to meet ya, Gust is it?"

The man returned his handshake. "Yep, Gust, Gust Schirmer. Nice to meet you, too."

One of the dark haired little girls stepped forward. "Daddy, who is he?"

Myrt answered. "This is your big brother, Ella Maude, his name is Sonny." She pointed to each child as she said the names. "This here is Ella Maude, this is your brother Jimmy, this is Ivy and." She took the baby from her husband. "This is mine and Gust's little one, Martha."

Gust said, "No need to stand on the porch all night."

Tommy stepped inside the house and heard a child's voice behind him. "Hi Grandma and Paw Gummalt. I got me a new big brother."

As soon as he sat down on the couch, all three kids came running toward him.

"I get to sit in his lap," said Ivy.

"No, I do," Ella replied.

"Damn-it Ella Maude, I said it first."

The little one was feisty. He could see who ruled the roost, and her language was bad, but cute. Jimmy was quiet and took a seat next to him. If he'd been any closer, he'd have been in his lap, too. The young boy had a natural smile in his eyes, and looked like Red with black hair. Boy was he ever a Kizziah.

It only took a look from Gust, and a few words from their mother and the children settled down.

"You kids leave Sonny alone, I'm sure he tired."

"Oh, it's okay, Myrt, but I'd like to ask you to call me Tommy. I've gone back to using my real name of Tommy Kizziah.

"Tommy what?" Ivy asked.

"Kizziah. That's your name, too."

"No, my name is Ivy Rogers."

"Hey." Myrt gave the baby back to Gust and picked Ivy up off of Tommy's lap. "I thought I told you kids to go to bed earlier. And Ella, why do you still have your clothes on?"

"When you saw the car coming and told us to go to bed, Mamma, well, I went to bed, but didn't change into my sleep shirt. I was too excited to see who it was."

"Oh, I see." Myrt gestured toward the back of the house. "You can go get your shirt on now. All three of you are going to sleep in the back room tonight, and Tommy can have Jimmy's room. Go."

He didn't know how any of the three could see where they were going; they were all staring at him as they walked away. He stomped his foot and lunged toward them. "Boo."

Laughter filled the air as their little feet scurried out of the room. Those were his siblings. How about that? The year of 1942 was his year for family reunion, and he liked it.

The Gummalts left, Myrt put the baby to bed and Gust took his leave to bed as well. Tommy was glad for the time alone with Myrtle. He'd forgotten how much he liked her.

Myrt settled into a chair across from him and they began to talk. It was like they'd never been apart. She listened while he told her of his life in South Carolina after she and Lon left. She was disappointed that he and Maggie didn't marry and didn't understand why they didn't, but he wasn't going to tell her that part.

He took a deep breath. "Okay, enough about me. Tell me what happened after Jimmy was born and you and Paw moved. I'm sorry I never got to come see y'all before you left South Carolina."

"That's okay, you're here now. Let me see, after Jimmy was born we moved to Rockwood, Tennessee, of course. I loved it there. Your Grandma Lyd was so good to me. Ella and Jr. were born there."

He hadn't thought of the other boy, Ella's twin. "Where is Jr.?"

A tear twinkled in her eye. "He died last year in 1941, just before Gust and I got married. Stepped on a rusty nail and got lockjaw. There was nothing we could do. He didn't tell me about the nail until it was too late and he was already too sick."

"I'm sorry to hear that, Myrt."

"Me, too, but we both know these things happen." She sighed. "Then your Paw got a sore throat in '36'. It finally went away, but he started to lose his voice. Someone told us about a place in DeQueen, Arkansas, that might be able to help him, so we packed up and moved there in February of nineteen-thirty-seven. I was pregnant with Ivy.

When we got there, the doctors told him there wasn't anything they could do. We lived in the park, and a month after we moved, Ivy was born."

"You live in the park?"

"Yep, inside the tent. And I had Ivy in that tent, too. Your daddy helped me have her. He was weak, and had lost a lot of weight, but he never complained. Ivy came with no trouble and in a couple of day's I was up and around again."

Lon kept playing the fiddle, harmonica, guitar and accordion as usual, but he couldn't sing anymore. Everyone there called him Arkansas Sam. He made his own tonic to sell to the folks. They liked it, too. That's how he made us a living. I made all the sign's for him, just like I did for the Foxhorns."

"Yeah, you sure have pretty handwriting, Myrt."

"Thank you, Tommy. When Ivy was five months old, we moved to a small trailer on the Montgomery's land. Mr. Montgomery and your paw set up the tent outside and Lon kept making his tonic. He was such a good salesman, he wouldn't be gone long before he'd have to come home and make another batch."

Then one day in December, he went to the Post Office to send Lyd a letter. He wasn't feeling good and I told him the letter could wait a couple of days, but he went anyway. He collapsed on the floor of the Post Office. Everyone in town knew you're Paw, so a couple of the men that were there took him to the motel and put him in the bed."

She wiped a tear from her cheek. "By the time I got there he could hardly raise his head. He told me he loved me and then he was gone." She met his gaze. "He was a good man, Tommy, a real good man."

He felt like he needed to change the subject. The last thing he wanted was for her to really start crying and it looked as if that's where she was headed.

"Yes, he was a good man. T.J. and Mary didn't even know he was gone."

She wiped her nose with a handkerchief. "Who?"

"My little brother and sister. T.J. and Mary."

Her brow furrowed. "I didn't know about them."

"They never lived with us after Maw got really sick. They

stayed with a couple of families in Texas. Mary was the only girl out of all of us kids."

"Your daddy never told me about no other kids. Only you. How many kids are there?"

He laughed. "Ten all together, countin' your three." Her look of astonishment tickled him.

"Ten!"

"Yep, there's Ike, Jack, Bill, Red, me, Mary and T.J."

"I thought Ike, Jack, Bill and Red were your Paw's brothers."

"He pulled one over on you, Myrt, they were his sons. He just didn't want you to know how old he was for fear you wouldn't marry him. And he was mighty taken with you."

She smiled. "That rat! How old was your Paw?"

"He was close to fifty when y'all married."

"If he wasn't already dead and buried right now, I'd kill him."

She began to laugh and he was glad her mood had lightened before they decided to bed down. Myrt showed him to a small room with only a bed and chest of drawers in it. Anything was good enough for him as long as he could get some sleep.

Morning did come early and the happy voices of children woke him. He joined them in the kitchen where breakfast was on the table.

"Good morning, Tommy, did you sleep good?" Gust asked.

"Sure did. I think I was out before my head hit the pillow."

"How long are you going to stay with us?"

"I'm gonna stay around for a little while this mornin', then I'll be on my way."

After they ate, Myrt's husband gave him a tour of their little farm. He went to the barn with Gust and the little ones. Ivy was only five, definitely spirited and, man, could she cuss. He'd never heard a little girl with a mouth like that. Ella seemed to want to make excuses for her little sister.

"I'm sorry you have to listen to Ivy say those bad words. She learns them from my daddy. He cusses during the day, then reads the Bible to us at night. I guess he thinks that makes it all better."

"You never know, Ella, Maybe it does."

He didn't have much of a chance to get to know his youngest siblings very well before he had to leave, but he'd be seeing them again.

With their goodbyes said; his heart was touched when Ella began to cry as he got into his car to leave.

She ran to him, gave him a big hug and said, "I'm going to pray every night that I get to see you again."

"Don't you worry, I'll be back someday."

Myrt took Ella by the hand. "Come on, let your brother go. He'd got to go to Lubbock and play some music."

1930's

Myrtle Gummalt

Lon

Tom at
different ages

Lon

Tom & friend.
Boys will be boys

Tom & Maggie

Lon, Tommy, Janie & Mary

Lon & Myrt

Jimmy & twins
Ella & Elick Jr.

Ella Maude

Girls from Medicine Show

Lon., Mary & Neighbor girl

1940's

Tommy and his
Army buddies,
1942

Reuben, Mary, Mary Lou & Tom

Ike's daughter
Dorothy

Baby Mary
Lou

Reuben & Mary Allen

Mary & Tom with new guitar

Reuben, Mary
& Mary Lou

Standing: Red, Bill & Jack
Sitting: Ike, Mary & Tommy

Ike & Tommy

T.J.

Red   Ike   Mary   Bill   Jack

T.J., Mary, Al, Mary Lou & Tommy

Tommy, Al & T.J.

Tommy's Car

Tommy, Jack, Red, Mary, Ike & Bill

Tommy

Ike & wife Thelma - Tommy & Thelma

Tommy & Jack

Ella, Maude & Ivy

Ivy & Jimmy
Kizziah

Martha Schirmer

Dealva, Bill & Jessie

Red & Frankie

Virgie,
Bill's wife

Tommy

Tommy, Bill & Red

Jack & Tommy

Tommy & Darlene
(Red's daughter)

Reuben &
Mary Allen

Drunk Indians Tommy & Ike

Myrtal & Gusp

Isom & Lena Collier

Arlene, MArgaret, Red, Trina, Dealva & Darlene

CHAPTER 8

Winter 1943

Tommy stepped up to the microphone and his voice boomed over the loud speakers, "Well, good evenin' folks. It's good to be here with ya.

"With New Year's Eve fallin' on a Thursday, y'all get a long weekend, and in just a few hours we'll be bringin' in the new year of 1944! How about that?!" The crowd of over five hundred roared in an explosion of applause. No matter how many times he heard it, the sound of their support made his heart skip. That was what it was all about.

"Now, wha-da-ya-say we get on with the music?" Again the people sounded their approval. "Jack, why don't you start us out with a little ditty on that fiddle."

His older brother stepped up to his microphone. "You got it, Tom. Here's a breakdown for ya, folks." Jack drew his bow across the strings and the rhythm section followed his lead.

Tommy watched the crowd as they clambered onto the dance floor. He had fallen right into the groove of playing with Jack's band in Lubbock. Was it ever good to be reunited.

Jack's wife, Jessie Bell, took him into her home and treated him well. Their three kids, Jack Jr., Janie Bell and Jo Ann, whom everyone called Jody, were like his own and he loved each and every one of them.

Red and his wife Essie May didn't seem to get along too well, but they had a cute little girl, Rebecca Jean. She spent a lot of time at Jack and Jessie's house.

The music stopped and again he addressed the crowd. "That was a good one, wasn't it? Ah, yes, we're gonna slow it down for ya' right now with a nice waltz."

The men chose their partners and the dance floor filled again. It was that way the entire night. Now, it was only five minutes until midnight. "Okay, folks, it's almost time for 1944!" Jessie joined Jack on stage, as did the other wives, to kiss their husbands and bring in the New Year. A pretty young lady named Nonie had approached him earlier in the evening and when he told her he didn't have anyone to kiss, she volunteered. He had a hard time accepting the idea that the ladies loved musicians, and he was always being propositioned. However, he wasn't complaining.

With Nonie by his side, he began the countdown. "Are you ready?" he asked the people who filled the hall. Their response echoed through the building. "1944, here we come!" He glanced at his watch. For only moments silence filled the room. Then he began, ,10,9,8,7,6," The people joined in the countdown. ,5...4...3...2...1...Happy New Year!"

Confetti looked like multi colored snow in the air. Noisemakers whirred, clattered and clinked. The band members gave short kisses to their ladies, then played Auld Lang Syne. The celebration threatened to raise the roof, but he heard Nonie's whispered words clearly.

"I'll meet you out front when you're done. We can go to my place."

Her smile was inviting, and he didn't turn her down. Nodding his agreement, he began to sing as she stepped off the bandstand. "Should old acquaintance be...

Summer 1945

While he waited in front of Jack's house, tumbleweeds blew across the road and the brown landscape faded into itself. He'd forgotten how much he disliked the flat, dry plains of

West Texas. The state had some beautiful places; they just weren't located in the western part.

What did he care? His brothers were there and he was playing music. That in itself compensated for trees and green grass. His breathing was better there, too.

His move to Lubbock in nineteen forty-two was a good one. Lubbock offered more opportunity, and being in a bigger city also helped, now that he didn't have a car. He thought he'd never sell it but he needed the money. In the last couple of months, he found himself borrowing Jack's car or hitching rides from his friends and band members. It wasn't so bad, but it got under his skin to have to depend on others.

That day, the drummer, Darrel, was going to give him a ride to a local radio station. He'd been asked to do three fifteen-minute radio shows every week for the station. It was a fun life and, as Darrel pulled up he realized he was truly blessed. He only needed one thing... a car.

The ride to the radio station was short, and he wasn't due to go on the air for half and hour, but he needed to get tuned up. Every time he went into the small studio, he was reminded of his days with Jimmy Rogers. The equipment was more sophisticated and reached a bigger audience, but the atmosphere of the broadcast room was the same. It was amazing how much things could change in fifteen years, but still remain the same.

He'd grown up a lot in those years, and was determined to make something out of his music. Right now, he felt he was well on his way to fulfilling his dream of being a popular Western singer. What more could he ask for?

"Want me to wait, Tommy?" Darrel asked.

"If you don't mind, I'd appreciate it."

"Okay, think I'll sit out here and smoke while you're on."

"I won't be long."

When he walked into the station, the receptionist handed him some letters.

"Looks like you have some fans out there, Tommy."

He glanced down at the envelopes and thumbed through them. They all had his name or the name of the band on them.

"Hells bells, what do you know about that? The Texas Dusters and I have fan mail." He couldn't believe it. He'd have Jessie read them to him later. Right now, he had to get ready for his spot.

* * *

The radio show had gone well the day before, and Tommy was ready for Saturday night. He liked to watch the hall fill with people as he and the guys tuned up. Some of the regulars he knew, but some were there for the first time. He made it a point to meet as many of the folks as possible, and tonight was no different. He needed to mingle.

He enjoyed himself while he made his way from table to table, but now it was time to start the dance. The first hour-long set would be for the dance hall crowd alone, then the band would take a fifteen-minute break and get ready for the thirty minute live radio show set. After that, each set would be forty-five minutes with fifteen-minute breaks in between.

Man, what kind of job was that? Work less than an hour, get a fifteen-minute break and get to smoke cigarettes and drink beer. What a deal. However, he didn't think of it as a job, he loved what he did and tried to make it fun for everyone.

He watched for his cue from the radio engineer. During the radio portion of the show, a young woman caught his eye. He'd never seen her there before, but boy, she was a looker.

A tiny little thing with dark hair and eyes, and man could she cut a rug. She was sitting with another dark haired girl. They were both nice looking, but for some reason, he couldn't take his eyes off her. And as much as she was dancing, it was apparent a lot of other guys couldn't either.

At break time, he made it a point to approach the table where the girls were seated. "Evenin' ladies. Do y'all have a special song you want to hear tonight?"

One of the girls met his gaze. "Anything you sing is fine with us."

He looked directly at the pretty little brunette. "Where ya from."

Her bright smile lit up the dim room, but her glance downward told him she was shy. Though her voice was faint, he understood her words.

"Meadow, but I live here in Lubbock now."

"I'm glad you live here. Meadow would be a pretty good ways for you girls to drive." He pulled out the empty chair next to her. "You mind it I sit down?"

She shook her head and he took a seat. "What's your name, hon?"

Grinning, she briefly met his gaze. "Frances, but my friends call me Frankie and my family calls me Tish. My daddy gives us all nicknames and Tish is mine."

Those sparkling brown eyes did something to his heart. He couldn't explain it, but he had to get to know this young woman better. "And this other lady is?" He glanced at the girl sitting beside her.

"My sister, Betty."

"Nice to meet y'all. Have you been to the Brown Derby before?"

"Yes," Frankie said, "Well, only a couple of times. Betty's been here more often. I figured she might be here and I just got a new car, so I came over to find her. We like your music. I listen to you on the radio all the time."

He wondered why he'd never noticed Frankie before. She was so sweet and one of the prettiest girls he'd ever seen. And, she had transportation! "A car, that's what I need. Mine went kaput on me here while back."

This could be his best opportunity to get to know Frankie better. He decided to take the plunge. "Would you mind to give me a ride home tonight after the dance?"

She gave her sister a quick look. "Betty?"

"Fine with me. I have my own car."

"Well, I guess I can. My sister Shirley's watching my boys tonight, so I can be a little late I guess. They'll all be in bed time I get home anyway."

"Boys?"

"Yes, I have two little boys. Johnny and Benny."

Funny, he hadn't noticed a wedding ring, however he hadn't been looking. He glanced at her left hand. Yep, there was one there all right. She didn't seem like the type that would take off her wedding band and have a fling with a stranger, nor have children out of wedlock. Damn.

With only a few long strides, he was at the stage. He moved with grace for a man his size. He had to be at least six foot three. Heck, she was only five foot two.

The times she'd been at the Brown Derby before, she'd noticed him, but never like tonight. Something was different. Surely it wasn't because he'd talked to her. However, his deep voice, did give her goose bumps when he called her "Hon."

Oh, that was ridiculous. She was acting like a high school girl that the quarterback had just talked to. But that's how she felt, and when Tommy started singing, her heart skipped a beat.

"Frankie...Frankie!"

Betty's voice penetrated her thought. "Yeah?"

"What the heck's wrong with you? Your eyes are glazed over and you're staring at Tommy Kizziah. You're not getting a crush on him, are you? He's probably just looking for a one-night stand. Girls flock around him all the time. Why would you think he'd pick you?"

Betty had a way of bringing reality back into view. She'd always had that knack. She was probably right, he just wanted her to take him home to see how far he'd get, but she had a surprise in store. Although she'd been married, her ex-husband to be was the only man she'd been with, and she'd have to get married again to be with another. She just wasn't that kind of girl. If that ruined her chances with Tommy, then she didn't want him anyway.

* * *

The ride to Jack and Jessie's was fun. Too bad he didn't have his own apartment. Tommy liked the way Frankie laughed at his corny jokes. Her smile brightened up the night. She was a delightful young woman and he really liked her. "This is it," he said, and she pulled to the curb.

"Hey, I loved your singing tonight. You've got the best band around here."

"Well, I thank ya', hon. I try to do my best. You can sure cut a rug on the dance floor, too. Man, where did you learn to dance like that?"

"I have two brothers and eight sisters. When we were little, we used to listen to the radio and dance all the time. We kind of taught ourselves, with Mamma and Daddy's help, of course."

"What does your daddy do?"

"He farms some, but he's a lawman. Mostly Mamma and the kids take care of the farm."

"And what do you do?"

"Well, right now, my sister Betty and I work at the drug store downtown, but I want to be a nurse someday."

"A nurse, that's nice." Moonlight glistened from her big, beautiful brown eyes. He fought the urge to kiss her. He didn't want her to be a one-night stand, and he didn't want to scare her. This one was special. Besides, his impression was that she wasn't the kind of girl that would go for that anyway. But he had to kiss her. The urge was too strong.

"Frankie, do you think...would you mind if I give you a good night kiss?" The slightest grin crossed the young woman's face.

"I guess that would be okay."

He scooted closer to the driver's side of the car, put his arm around her and when their lips met, it felt like they were made for each other. She allowed the kiss to linger just the perfect amount of time. He wanted more, but didn't dare ask. Why would he want to ruin what could possibly turn into something special with this sweet young thing?

He gazed down at her pretty face. "How old are you anyway?"

"Twenty one."

Young was right! "Twenty one, hells bells, you're just a pup." He took his arm from around her. Man, oh man, he was almost thirty. She was way too young for him, yet there was something that drew him to her.

"I am not. I've been married and have two kids. I have a job, a car, a new house and I know what I want in life. I'd say I'm pretty grown up."

"Yeah, I guess you are at that." He slid back towards the passenger door. "You must make pretty good money to have a new house, too."

"No, my in-laws, Mommy and Paw Jones, bought it for me. They don't believe in renting and they wanted their grandsons and me to have a nice place to live. They're really good people, and they don't like what their son has done to us."

It was none of his business about all that stuff. He didn't even know why he'd made the comment. "It's late and I'd better go in." He stepped out of the car, closed the door, walked around the front then over to her side and bent down to her opened window. "Can I see you again? I mean, I don't have a car I can come pick you up for a date with, but I'd really like to be with you again."

"Sure, I'll come back to the dance next Saturday night."

"Maybe after that, we can go out to breakfast or something. You'll have to drive, of course."

"Sounds good to me. It's a date."

His heart swelled in his chest. What did this little lady have that he couldn't resist? "Okay." He leaned into the window and gave her a little peck on the cheek. "See ya next week."

* * *

January 1946

It had only been a few months since he'd met the beautiful little Frances Jones, but he was in love. She was the best thing that had ever happened to him. Her fun loving yet grounded personality was one of the things he loved the most. Plus, she was a looker.

He even liked her two little boys Johnny and Benny. They seemed to like him okay, too. Johnny had fair skin and blond hair and looked like his Daddy, Red Jones, the other was olive skinned and had dark hair like Frankie. He hadn't met the boys' daddy yet, but he knew that the man wasn't any too nice to Frankie and he didn't like that.

Why would anyone want to run around on her or direct violence at her? He didn't know, but he knew he never would. She was the sweetest person he'd ever known.

She got along fine with Jack and Jessie. Jessie especially liked her and so did the kids. It seemed important to her to be liked by his family.

He rounded the corner going into Jack and Jessie's kitchen. "Hey, Jack, can I borrow your car? I'm gonna go down to the drug store and see Frankie."

"Sure, Tom, but what are you going to do about a car when me and Jessie move to Oregon in March?"

"I'll figure something out. I'm hoping I'll be married by then. We'll see." He took the keys from his brother. "I won't be long."

Jack smiled. "Yeah, yeah, yeah, that's what you said yesterday when you went to see Frances, and three hours later you showed up. You're going to pop the question today?"

"Yep, I am. What can I say, brother? I just can't stay away from her."

"That's well and good and I'm glad you finally found somebody, but don't forget we've gotta play tonight at the Derby, so be home early so we can get set up."

How could he forget they were going to play? "I won't."

"Good, then go and have a good time."

That's just what he was going to do. After the dance that night, he planned to ask Frankie to marry him. He knew she wasn't divorced yet, but hopefully she would be soon.

Even though she and her husband had been separated for quite some time, she couldn't afford the legalities. However when the man contacted something contagious from another woman and Frankie found out about it, she vowed the paper work would get done soon.

When he reached the drugstore and went inside, there she was. Pretty as a picture, the love of his life stood behind the soda fountain counter. He saw a twinkle in her eye when she noticed him. That was another thing he loved about her. She always seemed to be glad to see him. It made his heart sing.

He pulled off his coat, hung it on the rack by the door, took a seat at the end of the counter and waited for her to finish with another customer. She always looked nice, but today her dress fit her a little tighter then usual and showed off a small waist and all of her curves.

One of these days, if he had his way about it, she would be his wife and that curvaceous body would be his. He knew it wouldn't happen before they were married, but that was okay, too. The best things always come with time.

"Howdy." He took her hand when she approached.

"Hi."

"You gonna come to the dance tonight?"

"I don't think so. Johnny wasn't feeling well when I left this morning. He had a little bit of a fever, so I think I'd better stay home with him."

Oh, no, what was he going to do? This was the big night. "Well, won't he be okay without you for even a little while?"

"Tommy, I've been away from him all day. He needs his mother. He's sick."

He couldn't argue with that. She was an attentive mother and that was another thing that pulled at his heartstrings. "Okay, I understand." He'd just have to change his plans.

The other guy sitting at the bar left. Frankie picked up the mess, got a couple of sodas then took a seat beside him.

"I really wish I could go tonight, but..."

Pressing his fingers gently to her lips he shushed her. "It's okay, really, I understand." He took both of her hands in his. "I have something to ask you." Damn, this was harder then he thought. His heart was beating in his throat and his breath threatened to catch there as well. He'd never been this nervous before.

He pulled a deep breath into his lungs then let it out slowly. Meeting the gaze of her big brown eyes calmed him and he knew this was the woman he wanted to spend the rest of his life with. It was time. "Frankie, I love you and want you to marry me." There, said and done.

The look on her face was one he'd never seen before. He could read it well. She kindly drew her hands from his. This wasn't going to be good.

Frankie knew her actions had already told Tommy her answer, but she had to explain. He didn't know how much she loved him. "Tommy, I-I don't know what to say? I'm flattered that you want me to be your wife, b-but I'm just not ready to take on another marriage right now. I mean...I'm not even out of the first one."

The look on his face made it clear, she was breaking his heart and that was the last thing she wanted to do. Never before had her feelings for a man been this strong, but she had so many things to consider. And she didn't want to take the chance of getting hurt again.

Tommy was a well-known musician that women were after

all the time. Even though he'd never given her any reason not to trust him, there was still doubt in her heart. It was because of Dennis' infidelity, she knew, but she couldn't get over it. Maybe in time, but not now, not yet.

"I don't mean right away."

His hazel eyes reflected his feelings and she couldn't stop her tears. "I know, but I can't say yes. Maybe another time, but not right now." She looked down at her hand where she still wore the ring from her failed marriage. Even though she and Dennis Jones were separated, she was still married to him. Tommy's warm fingers under her chin lifted her head to meet his gaze.

"Hey, I'm the one who's supposed to be crying here, not you."

How could she turn him down? Was she crazy? Most of the women in Lubbock would say yes to him on the spot! Her tears flowed even more readily at his compassion.

"You said maybe another time so that gives me hope. I'll just keep trying. When you're ready, you'll let me know. Don't worry, I'm not going to give up on you."

A customer walked in the front door. She grabbed a napkin, dried her tears and stood. "No, don't give up on me.

Someday I'll be ready for marriage again, and I can't think of anyone I'd rather be with."

She wondered if her saying no would stop their relationship now. Maybe he wouldn't want to see her until she was ready to get married, and by that time, he might find someone else. Then what would she do. Oh, she was so confused.

Walking around the counter she placed a fake smile on her face. "May I help you?" she asked the woman sitting on a stool.

"I'll have a vanilla milkshake, please."

"Okay." She turned her back. The air that rushed out of the freezer felt good on her face. The ice cream was hard as she pulled the scoop across the top. The woman's voice drifted to her ears.

"Say, aren't you Tommy Kizziah?"

"Yes, ma"Am I sure am."

The woman giggled like a little school-girl, then got up to take the seat next to Tommy. Frankie's blood warmed in her veins and jealousy crept up in her heart.

"Well, well, you are just as good-looking up close as you are on that stage. Mmm, mmm, mmm, tall, dark and handsome, I like my men like that. And I really like the music you make. I bet we could make some good music together, you and me."

A dull ache made its way from Frankie's jaw into her head. She'd never clenched her teeth together so hard, but she had to, to keep her mouth shut. What she really wanted to do was slap that sorry satchel off the bar stool. How could a woman act so— so— darn, it infuriated her! But she realized she couldn't say a thing because she'd turned down Tommy's proposal and didn't even know if they'd be seeing each other anymore.

Forcing herself not to slam the milky drink onto the counter top, she placed it in front of the woman. "That'll be thirty-five cents." Her stomach churned and she held her tongue when she saw the goo goo eyes the woman was giving Tommy. It was one of the hardest things she had ever done, but she had to remember she was a lady and this person in front of her was definitely not!

When the customer dug in her purse for her money, Tommy stood up. "Well, I'd better go."

Frankie glanced up at him and knew by the amusement in his eyes, her face told her mood. "Ah, Frances, would you come over here, please?"

What was he doing? Didn't he know if she got any closer to that woman she might lose her cool? She took a deep breath and went around the counter to stand beside him. She didn't take her gaze from him because she didn't want to meet the one of the woman. He was so tall and handsome, and she was somewhat comforted when he put his arm around her shoulder.

"Ma'am," he said to the other woman, "I'm really glad you like my music, and I appreciate you coming out to see me, but you see this little lady right here? She's gonna' be my wife someday. You're a nice person and all, but I love Frances here. She's the only one I'll be makin' music with anywhere else but on the band stand."

Her heart swelled with even more love for this man, if she could love him more. Why was he doing and saying this even after she said no to his offer? Now she was confident that she could look at the woman. Laughter fought to get out when she saw how flushed the woman's face was. Poor thing realized she'd just made a butt of herself.

"Wa, er, ah, I-I'm sorry, I didn't know you were spoken for." She placed her money on the counter and without taking a sip of her shake, left the drugstore.

Tommy said, "That's one fan that probably won't be back at the dance."

"She probably won't ever come in here again either. But, why'd you tell her we were going to get married?"

"Because I have confidence that one day, you'll say yes."

He was probably right. A grin lifted the corners of her mouth. "We'll see."

"I'd better go. I'm sorry you're not going be at the dance tonight. Can I have a little kiss before I go."

"Does this mean that we're going to still see each other even though I said no?"

"Why, hells bells, I said I'm not going to give up, and I'm not. You're my girl as far as I'm concerned. Now how "Bout that kiss."

She glanced around and her sister Betty, who also worked there, was the only other one in the store. She was cleaning some shelves. What could a kiss hurt?

CHAPTER 9

May 1946

Damn, Tommy couldn't believe he was leaving the woman he loved behind to move to Oregon. Jack and Jessie had made the move two months earlier, and when he got his brother's call saying the Country Western music was booming on the West Coast, he couldn't pass it up.

Frankie and he seemed close, but even now she wouldn't marry him. He couldn't wait around for her to get her divorce finalized. She'd been talking about it, but as scarce as money was, there was no telling how long it would be. If only he could afford to give her the money, get it done and take her with him, but that wasn't going to happen. As it was, he had to borrow the money to make this move. Besides, she wouldn't go as long as she still had the name Jones. Hopefully, the cash situation would be better in the West.

Frances' priorities were always her sons, as it should be, and he respected her for that. He'd really miss her and the boys. He was attached to the two little fellows, and they felt like his own.

The tear stained face of his true love was etched into his mind. It was all he could do to leave her, but it was what he had to do and it was time. He needed to pursue his career, his dream, and he damn sure wasn't getting any younger. His thirtieth birthday was coming in December. Thirty. Man oh man, how time passed. He'd lived a lot in his lifetime. Been a lot of places, seen a lot of things. Overall he guessed he was blessed. However, he probably wouldn't fall in love again, and resigned that he'd never have children of his own.

He glanced out the window of the train. Brown land that spread for miles and miles sped by. It seemed like he could see to the other side of the world the prairie was so flat. Frances and the boys were the only things about West Texas he would miss.

* * *

October 1946

Tommy placed his empty beer bottle on the porch floor alongside a few others. Jack came out the door with two more. The air was cool, but, man, it was beautiful in Oregon.

Jack had a job at the Chemawa Indian school, and the School provided him and Jessie with a small but nice apartment on the pleasant little campus.

Thankfully Jack talked to the School board members and they hired him on, too. His job was to teach the kids about farming, how to run the tractors and how to take care of the orchards. It didn't pay much, but it was better than nothing and he appreciated it.

He still missed Frankie. They talked often and wrote letters back and forth. Well, he couldn't read or write, but Bill Suggs, Jessie's brother read her letters to him, and then would write her back for him.

He took the full beer from his brother. "Man, this is nice, brother. Even with the leaves falling off the trees, it's still pretty and green here."

"Yeah, quite a difference from Texas."

He leaned back in his straight-backed chair, lifted the front legs off the porch and rocked on the back ones. "Yep."

"Heard from Frankie lately?"

"Not in a few days. I asked her to marry me again the last time we talked. She said no. Said she's still not divorced."

"Well, I think you need to get your mind off her for a while. What say we go out tonight and hear some local bands."

He did need to hear some music. And, hells bells, he'd had just enough beer that going out tonight sounded pretty good. "Okay, let's do "Er."

* * *

The band had just started the last set of the night. When the second song was over, Buddy Simmons heard a commotion in the back of the dance hall. From the stage, he couldn't see exactly what was going on. He didn't think it was a fight, but a loud booming voice that seemed to be getting closer. It was hard to see into the crowd in the dim light, and then he noticed two tall Indian looking guys coming toward the bandstand.

"What the hell? Who is that?" Buddy could tell by the swagger in the two men's walk that they had been drinking their share of alcohol.

"I don't know, but I think we're fixing to find out," said Larry, who was the leader of the band and the owner of the hall.

"Howdy, y'all. I'm Tommy Kizziah and this is my brother Jack." He stepped up onto the stage. "We want to play a couple of songs if you don't mind."

Buddy was speechless and so it seemed was everyone else on the bandstand. These guys were big...and drunk...he damn sure wasn't going to say anything to them. If they thought they were musicians, more power to them. Let them play.

Larry's wife, Rose stepped up to the tall man who called himself Tommy. Hopefully she wasn't going to get herself into trouble, but they knew guys like this usually would take a scolding from a woman before they would a man.

"Excuse me, but—"

"Well now little lady, if you'll just let me borrow that guitar, I'll sing you a song." Tommy said.

Buddy couldn't believe his eyes. Rose took off her guitar

and handed it to the tall man. What kind of spell was she under?

"Jack, grab that boy's bass and let's pick somethin'"

The one named Jack stepped toward the bass player. He handed him the stand up bass guitar and stood back. Buddy had never seen anyone just come into a dance hall and take over the stage like these guys were doing. He wanted to see if they could play.

Tommy adjusted the microphone stand to fit his tall frame. His deep voice boomed out of the loud speakers. What a total change from the man who looked drunk as a skunk only seconds ago.

"Howdy there folks. I'm sorry about this little interruption in the music, but I'm gonna sing you a song." He turned toward the band. "In the key of C boys and simple two four time."

He turned his attention back to the microphone and strummed a C chord on the guitar. "My friends see me out a dancin'..."

Buddy had to force his mouth closed at the sound of the big man's voice. Boy could he sing. The band members fell in right with the time of the song and sounded like they'd been playing with this guy forever. He was impressed. No wonder the guy was confident enough to take over the bandstand. But that still didn't excuse his actions, or his brother's.

Applause cracked the air when the song was over. The crowd liked the guy. They really liked him. He hadn't heard a crowd make that much noise since last New Years Eve.

"This one's in A fellas."

Rose stayed on the stage and was standing by Buddy and his steel guitar.

Buddy tapped her shoulder and she leaned down to hear what he had to say. "Damn, what do you think about that?"

"I think they're good," Rose replied.

"Yeah they are, but I mean the way they just took over."

"It's never happened to me before, and I'm not sure I like them, but, man, can that guy belt it out."

Buddy was relieved when the end of the last set came. Tommy and Jack finished playing out the night. Now he could pack up and go home. He wasn't sure what to say to the two men. Actually, he wasn't going to say anything, he just wanted to get out of there and go home to Opal.

The two tall Indian-looking men already had another beer each. Man, they were drinkers. He did, however, overhear the men telling Larry and Rose thanks and sorry they barged in, but it had been a long time since they'd played together.

They didn't seem like bad fellows, just pushy. He wanted to avoid them, but obviously it wasn't going to be possible. Tommy approached with his hand extended. Buddy couldn't bring himself to be rude, so he accepted the shake.

"Thank ya for sticking in there with us on those songs. You do a mighty fine job on that steel. My brother mostly plays the fiddle but can plunk a bass pretty good to."

"You're welcome." He tried to turn his attention back to his business, but the man wouldn't let him.

"I'm Tommy Kizziah."

"Buddy."

"Say, I know we probably haven't made too good of an impression on you tonight, but my brother and I will be putting together a band soon and we'll need a good steel man. Do you have a phone number you can give me?"

Buddy was tempted to tell him no, or give him a wrong number, but he'd seen how the people reacted to this man's singing and showmanship. Did he want to pass up the opportunity to work with them? "Sure."

With some reserve, he gave Tommy his number. What would it hurt to talk to him? Especially if he was sober.

"Thanks again, I'll be calling ya."

Buddy packed up and got ready to head for home. It was a little bit of a drive back to Salem, and he was ready to get there. Tommy and Jack Kizziah came out of the building. Whew, they were loud and laughing and having a drunk ol' time. He hoped this wasn't a prelude to the way these guys acted all the time. He sure wouldn't play in their band if it were.

He got in his car and watched the other men's vehicle pull onto the road in front of him with Jack in the driver's seat. He didn't want to follow them, but it was inevitable that he'd have to.

Following their lead, he thought about the talented Tommy. Jack was no slouch on the bass either, but he hadn't done any singing. Tommy had done it all, even the fronting, which he was very good at as well.

What the hell was that? He saw something fly out of the window of Jack and Tom"S car. There it was again, only on the other side. He watched and in a few minutes it happened.

Damned, they were throwing out beer bottles!

The scenario happened at least three times before they got back to Salem, which was only about a thirty-minute drive. Those two guys could sure put away a lot of booze. Witnessing all that had happened at the club, now this, he wished he wouldn't have given out his number.

Tommy walked into the living room where his brother sat in his favorite chair. "Man, I feel bad today. My head's killing me, and my stomach's not feelin' that good either. Got any aspirin?"

"I'm in the same boat," Jack said getting up. "I'll get 'em. Jessie's fixing breakfast, so that will help, too."

He followed Jack to the bathroom. "Was she pretty mad at you?"

"Mad as a hornet, but she"Ll get over it. She always does."

"You do this often?"

"No, not really, but I have been known to pull a boner now and again."

"Well, I know I'm not going to make a habit of it. Hells bells. I've never gone up on another band's stage and taken over like we did last night." He couldn't believe he'd done that.

"Me neither, but it was kind of fun."

He had to admit, it was exciting. "Yeah, did you see the look on their faces when we first went up there?"

Jack chuckled. "Sure did."

It was something he enjoyed, but would never do again. "Well, we gotta keep up a good image around here if we expect to do anything in the music business. We can't do anymore of that kind of stuff."

"Yeah, I know. Here."

He accepted the white tablets from Jack. How could these two little things make him feel better? Only sleep would really cure what ailed him, and maybe a little food.

Tommy opened his eyes and glanced at the clock. Four o'clock. Hells bells, he'd slept all afternoon. He sat up on the side of the bed and realized he felt much better than the first time he woke up on that day.

He wished Frankie was there, to show her comforting smile and reassure him. Making an ass of himself the night before was something she wouldn't approve of, but somehow, she'd make him feel better about a bad thing. She just had that way about her.

They talked on the phone less and less lately and he'd resigned himself to the fact it was over between them. It was something he didn't want to accept, but had to. The past five months since he'd left her in Texas had passed quickly. He'd have thought that he'd be missing her less by now, but that wasn't the case.

Why, she'd saved all her spare money and since he'd been gone and put in her very own restaurant. She could work her own hours, and there was a little apartment above the cafe that she and her little ones lived in. She loved being home for them and being able to keep an eye on the mischievous tykes. No, she would never come to Oregon to be with him.

But, today a phone call to her was the medicine what he needed to make him feel better. Then after that, he would dial up that Buddy guy. He needed to put a band together as soon as possible. Maybe it would take his mind off of Frankie. He doubted it.

The receiver went back in its slot with ease when he hung up the phone. How great it was to hear the voice of the woman he loved, even knowing they had no future. Oh well, no use crying over spilled milk. It was time to move on.

He picked up the receiver again and dialed the number on the paper he held, then waited for an answer.

"Hello."

Hmm, a woman's voice, maybe Buddy was married. "Howdy. Is this the ah," Why hadn't he sounded out Buddy's last name before he called? Sometimes he felt like a dummy because he couldn't read. "S-Simmons house?" He hoped he got it right.

"Yes it is."

"Can I speak to Buddy, please ma"Am?"

"Yes, just a minute. Buddy, phone."

He waited a short while then heard the man's voice.

"Hello."

"Buddy, this is Tommy Kizziah. We met last night."

"Yeah. How could I forget?"

"Hey, first of all I want to apologize for acting like that last night. I've never done that kind of thing before and don't intend to make a habit of it."

"Well, that's good to know, Tom. I was kind of worried about that. I wished I hadn't given you my number after I saw all those beer bottles flying out the windows of your car on the way home."

He laughed at the thought of what the man might have witnessed. "Sorry about that. We must have been a sight, but rest assured, it won't happen again."

"You two fellow's got Indian blood in you?"

"Yeah, some Cherokee, why?"

"Just thought you looked like it, that's all. I guess I'll accept your apology and we can move on. What can I do for you?"

Poor guy, he must have thought they were a couple of drunken Indians that had come to take over the joint. He could imagine what the others thought, too.

"I appreciate that Buddy. Say, I'm going to put together a band and I'd like for you to play steel for me. I know you're working with someone, but I'd still like to have you."

"Where"D you come from, Tom?"

Tommy guessed he'd better tell this man his musical background. Maybe that would help him make the decision to join the group. Rather, become the third member of a forming band.

Starting from the top, he told Buddy about teaching himself to play, singing with Jimmy Rogers, working on the medicine shows, radio shows and about his maw. He relayed it all as quickly as possible, but the memories it brought back made him nostalgic. Sometimes he still missed Jimmy and he definitely missed his mother.

"...and that's what brought me to Salem. Knowing how strong Country Western music is here. What do you say? Will you think about it?"

"Yes I will, and I'll give you something to think about, too. Y'all made quite an impression on me last night. I don't mean the drinking, of course, I mean your talent. I could tell you'd been in show business for awhile. What are your future plans in the music business? You've moved around a lot."

"I have, but I'm here now and I'm staying. I want to do some recording. Play in all the best places. Get our own radio show. I want to do it all. I intend to make it big, and I'm going to do it from right here on the West coast."

"Sounds like you're a determined man."

"I am determined to be in the music business one way or another."

"That brings me to my proposal. Something for you to think about."

His curiosity was high. What was on Buddy's mind? "Go ahead."

"I talked to Larry and Rose earlier today. They were as impressed with your singing as I was. What would you think about not putting a band together but joining Rose and Larry's band? They have a bus to travel in, and we play all over the area. The money's not bad and you can start right away. You'd be playing rhythm guitar, singing and doing some front work."

This, he hadn't thought about. Joining an existing group? It was something for him to ponder. "What about Jack?"

"That's the bad thing. I know you want to work with him, but they can't use him. Not that he's not good, but for now, they don't need him."

"Well, I don't know about that. I'll talk to him about it and see what his reaction is." It would be nice to get that income started right away instead of looking for more guys and putting it together himself right now. "I'll tell you what, I'll think about that, you think about joining us and we'll talk tomorrow."

"That sounds like a plan."

"I'll call you in the morning."

"Okay, Tom."

He hung up and took a seat on the sofa. "Well, brother Jack, now we have something else to think about."

"Yeah, what's that?"

"Buddy just offered me a job working with the band he's playing with."

"You mean instead of us putting something together?"

"Yeah, only thing is they only want me. For now anyway."

Jack nodded and was quiet for only a moment. "You'd better take it."

"But what about you and the plans we've made."

"I've been meaning to talk to you about that today, but haven't had any time. Maybe this is the best thing that could have happened. I don't really want to play full time right now. I like my day job and need to concentrate on it for my family's sake. You, on the other hand, don't have any responsibilities, and you can travel or whatever you need to do. I'm never going to be a star, but you could be." He paused. "I say do it, Brother."

* * *

Fall 1948

Tommy raked the leaves on the Chemawa campus and reflected on the changes in his life since he'd been in Oregon. He worked with some great Indian kids from all over the country and from all tribes. They were hard workers and wanted to learn. He was proud of them.

He'd lost touch with Frankie about six months earlier. She probably had another boyfriend. Their letters and phone calls had gradually tapered off to nothing. However, music had occupied his time. He still missed her and thought of her often. The thoughts were getting fewer and farther in between.

He enjoyed playing with Larry and Rose, and was glad he and Buddy had become such good friends. Buddy's wife, Opal, was a sweetheart, too. He felt as close to Buddy as he did to his own brother. Life was going well. He was playing music, working full time at the Indian School and didn't have to travel every weekend.

A couple of months earlier, when Larry and Rose told him they had bought the Aumsville Pavilion in Aumsville Oregon, he was surprised. After they sold their other dance hall, he didn't think they'd ever have another one. But it was great they did. It was nice having a sit down playing job. No setting up and tearing down all the equipment every weekend anymore. That part of it was great.

He was concerned about Rose. She hadn't been feeling too good, but she kept right on going. Working in the band and running the hall were only a couple of things she did. She also did all the bookwork, and paid the members of the band and all the help.

"Tommy," A woman said from the office door. "You're wanted on the telephone."

"Who is it?"

"I don't know, some lady."

He leaned the rake against a tree and went inside. "Who'd be calling me here?"

"Don't ask me, but she sounds sweet."

He picked up the receiver. "Hello."

"Tommy?"

"Yeah." He recognized the voice as soon as she spoke his name and his heart skipped a beat.

"This is Frances."

"Hi, how'd you get this number?"

"I called Jessie and she gave it to me. I hope it's okay that I called."

"Sure it is. What's wrong?"

"Nothin's wrong. I-I was just thinking about you and want-ed to call. I heard a song on the radio the other day. One you used to sing to me, and I got to missing you."

"I'm glad you still think of me now and then. I think of you, too."

"Tommy, I'm ready to get married. I-if you still want me, that is."

Had he heard her right? She wanted to get married? How could he get her there? When could it happen? This was the best day of his life. He would go get her. That's what.

"Tommy, are you there?"

"You're not fooling around are you? You really want to get

married?"

"My divorce is final now. I sold my restaurant and have been working at the hospital as a nurse's aid. I'm at work, now. I love you and miss you and want to come to Oregon and be your wife."

"Yiiipppppeeeeee!" He saw the way the secretary looked at him. "I'm gonna marry the woman I love!"

"So you still want to get marry me, Tommy, after all this time?"

"Why, hells bells, Frankie, what do you think I've been waiting for. Of course I still want to marry you.

"I have some vacation time coming up soon. I'll try to figure something out on how to get you here, and I'll call you tonight. Is your number still the same?"

"Yes."

"Then you'll be hearing from me soon. I love you, baby."

"I love you, too."

He hung up the phone and glanced toward the woman taking care of the small office.

"Sounds like you're excited, Tom."

"Yes, ma"Am. She finally said yes after two years."

"I'm proud for you."

"Thanks, me too."

♪ SHARON KIZZIAH-HOLMES

CHAPTER 10

"This has been a pretty long trip, Jackie." Tommy looked across the car seat at his oldest nephew. "Sure glad your daddy's letting you go with me to Texas to pick up Frankie."

"Yeah, me, too. And I'm glad Hal's with us."

"Yep. Had to have someone drive my car back. I can't drive mine and Frankie's too." He glanced at his sleeping best friend. It was nice of Hal to volunteer to make the trip with him. He didn't know how he was going to get both cars back. He didn't want Frankie driving that whole way by herself. This way they'd at least have three drivers.

"I can't wait to see Grandpa and Grandma Suggs."

"I'll bet you can't. They're good folks."

"When are we going to be there?"

"This will be our last night on the road. We should pull into Lubbock tomorrow about noon. If we get an early start, that is.

"We'll be stopping soon to get a room. I'm beat and we all need some rest. Besides, I want to get a bath and look my best when I see Frankie. I hope she still thinks I'm handsome." He pretended to admire himself in the rear view mirror.

"You think you're handsome, Uncle Tommy, so why shouldn't she? You told me that all of the ladies think you're handsome."

"Now don't you go telling that to Frances, you hear me?"

Jackie smiled, "Hmmm, I don't know. That might cost ya."

"Yeah? Well, we'll see." He pulled into a small motel in a

little town in New Mexico. "Mess with me, and you'll pay for the room tonight." He ruffled Jackie's black hair. "Now, you wake Hal up and I'll go get us a room."

Looking out across the flat brown land, Tommy realized he didn't miss the West Texas desert at all. He just wanted to get Frankie and get back to Oregon.

Lubbock was in sight. It wouldn't be long until he'd hold his love in his arms once again. The closer they got, the more he fought to catch his breath. Man, his heart was racing, too. He had waited a long time for this. God willing, he wouldn't keel over with a heart attack before he got there.

When he pulled up to Frankie's sister's house, he put his hand to his chest, took a deep breath, swallowed hard and forced himself to calm down.

"Uncle Tommy, you all right?"

He must really looked stupid, a big guy like him acting a fool over a woman. Boy oh boy.

"Yeah, he's all right, Jackie." Hal got out of the car. "He just knows he's going to finally get in Frankie's britches, once they talk to the judge."

Tommy was going to kill him. "That's not it, Jackie. I'm just excited to get to see her, that's all. Let's go."

When Frankie came out of the house, he lost his breath completely. He walked toward her. Hells bells she was beautiful. Her bright smile, her hair shining in the sunlight, that cute little figure of hers, everything about her was even more perfect than he remembered.

She met him in the middle of the yard, and for a minute, he couldn't say anything. He just stared at her. In a few days this woman would be his wife. His wife! "Yehhoooo!" He picked her up, and she put her arms around his neck as he twirled around. "Hello, Mrs. Kizziah!"

"Hello, Mr. Kizziah."

When he stopped, he met her gaze. Her brown eyes twinkled. "You sure are pretty." He placed his lips to hers. Oh, how he'd missed her sweetness. He gently put her down and the kiss lasted until her feet touched the ground. He didn't want to ever let her go and hugged her in his arms until Jackie's voice caught his attention.

"Uncle Tommy, you're drawing a crowd." Jackie nodded toward the house.

He glanced in that direction. Standing in the doorway was Frankie's sister, holding the hands of Johnny and Benny. He smiled down at Frankie. "I guess we are." Quickly, he brushed her lips with his once again and let her go. When he stepped free, the two little boys ran to him.

"Tommy!" Johnny said.

"Tommy!" Benny chimed in.

"Well, if it ain't Pete and repeat!" He picked up Johnny then Benny and hugged them both. They were going to strangle him if they squeezed his neck any harder. "You boys been good to your mamma?"

A smile reached all the way across Johnny's little freckled face. "Yes we have. We've missed you, Tommy. Mamma says we're going to live with you in an organ. How are we all going to fit in it?"

Laughter bubbled out of him and he was helpless to stop it. He realized he'd almost given up something very precious to him. His family! Frances, Johnny and Benny. He loved them all!

"Now you boys leave Tommy alone. I'm sure he's tired from such a long drive." Frankie took Benny out of his arms.

He put Johnny down and squatted down so he could see their faces. "Not an organ, Johnny, Oregon. It's a state, just like Texas is a state, but it's called Oregon."

"Is it big enough for all four of us?"

"I think so, Son."

"Y'all go on now and play with Jackie." Frankie tried to shoo them away.

"But I want to stay with Tommy, Mamma."

"You'll have the rest of your life to be with Tommy. Now do as I said."

"Yes, ma'am."

Tommy put his arm around her waist and walked her into the house. It was good to have her by his side again.

Frankie sat on the sofa and he sat beside her. "What are your plans, Tommy?"

"I plan to get married."

Her smile showed her dimples. "I know that. I mean, when, how?"

"I have to take Jackie to Spur to see Jessie's folks. I thought we could go to Oklahoma City, see my brother Ike and get married there. We'll drop Jackie off on the way."

"When are you planning on leaving?"

"Is tomorrow too soon?"

She laid her head on his chest. "Not soon enough for me."

He pulled her close. "Tomorrow it is, then."

* * *

"Tommy, I'm not going to stay at Ike's ex wife's house for three days until we get married. I don't even know that woman. I won't impose on her like that."

"Baby, I didn't know we'd have to wait three days. Why won't you stay here with Ike and me?"

"I told you that I'm not sleeping with you until we're married."

"We don't have to sleep together. I'll sleep on the couch and you can sleep in Ike's spare bedroom."

"No, what will everyone think? I'll tell you what they'll think. They'll think we're sleeping together. I'm just going to catch a bus back to Lubbock and when you get your visit out, you come back and get me. We can get married then."

He could see it would be useless to argue with her. "If that's what you want to do, then that's what we'll do. I just think it's silly, that's all."

The trip to the station was quiet, but before the bus left, he took her in his arms. "I love you, and I'm sorry about the mix up."

She returned his embrace. "I'm sorry I feel so strongly about this. I know it's not your fault. You couldn't have known. Anyway, it'll be all right. We'll be married soon enough."

He kissed her one last time before she got in the vehicle. Black smoke billowed out of the bus's exhaust as it pulled away. "Soon, and forever, my love." He waved goodbye, but this time it wouldn't be for long.

Frankie put her hands on her hips. "Tommy, what in the world happened to your hair?"

He saw for the first time what his wife to be looked like when she was angry. She was cute as a bug. "I cut it off into a flat top. What's the matter, Baby, don't you like it?" He reached to pull her to him, and she slapped his hand away.

"No, I don't. All my beautiful black curls are gone. I don't like it, and right now I don't like you. I don't think I'll even marry you looking like that." She crossed her arms and turned away.

He tried to stop the chuckle that forced its way out. "Ah, Frankie, it's just hair. It'll grow back, I promise." He turned her to face him. She looked like a little girl with her pouting bottom lip.

"I guess you're right, but it doesn't make me like it any better. And get that smile out of your eyes, I'm trying to stay mad at you."

"Come here." He pulled her into his arms. "Let's go get married. Right now."

"I'd love to, but it's Saturday. There not any place we can go on the weekend."

He lightly kissed her lips. "Then, what do you say we head

for Oregon. We can tie the knot there."

"Well, I guess there's nothing stopping us. You've already picked up Jackie from Spur, I went to Lovington and got the boys and said goodbye to Mamma and Daddy."

"What were the boys doing in Lovington?"

"Betty took them over so they could spend time with the Jones' and Mamma and Daddy."

"Oh, I see. So we can leave in the morning then?"

"Yes, but don't think we're going to get a motel room together while we're on the road."

He knew her better then that. She had her mind made up they weren't going to make love before they were married, and he respected her for that. "When we have to stop for the night, I'll get a room for me and Jackie and one for you and the boys.

* * *

The second day on the road, morning came quickly and Tommy was glad to be half way through the second leg of their trip. They made good time all day long the day before and it looked like this day would be the same.

The boys and Jackie seemed to be enjoying each other when they weren't sleeping. Thankfully, Jackie had taken on the roll of caregiver for the two young ones. It gave Frankie and him some time together, even if they were all in the same car.

He knew today would be a little more trying than the day before. They were about to start through the hot desert, but they'd make the best of it. Before it was over, they'd see a lot of different countryside. He hoped Frankie enjoyed the journey.

Johnny's voice came from the back seat. "Hey, Mamma, how come the road is so skinny here?"

"Because it's only one lane, Son."

"Well, what if cars come from the other direction?"

"See that little jig in the road there?"

"Yes."

"That's called a pull-off. We'll find one every couple of miles." If another car is coming, we'll be able to see them and we or they will pull onto that little jig and let the other one by."

"Oh, I see. That's neat."

Tommy thought it was good, too, except for the fact it really slowed down the traveling time. He peered across the vast expanse and the view went on and on. He'd bet you could see for five miles in every direction, not unlike the prairie of West Texas. He couldn't see the end of this stretch of road yet, but he knew it was out there somewhere.

The jaunt across the flatlands yesterday, was over late in the afternoon when they stopped once again for the night. They were getting close to home. It was the beautiful Cascade Mountains in Oregon he couldn't wait for his bride to be to see. Now they were right in the middle of them.

Jackie was taunting Johnny and Benny. "There are bears out there, you know."

Tommy watched in the rear view mirror as the two young boys studied the hillside.

"Yes, there are, and deer, too." Jackie put one hand on top of each boy's head and pushed them down in the seat so they couldn't see out the window. "See, there's a bear now."

He laughed as Jackie over-powered them and held them steady. Johnny and Benny both fought like hell to get up to see the bear.

"Let me go!" Johnny said.

"Mamma, I want to see the bear!" Benny pleaded.

"Look how big that bear is, Uncle Tommy," Jackie teased.

The struggle was fierce, until finally the older boy let them go.

Johnny popped up in the seat and looked frantically out the window. "Where? Where is he?"

With a sigh, Jackie answered. "Sorry, he's gone already."

"You did that on purpose, Jackie. That's not fair."

"Did what?"

"Held us down so we couldn't see the bear."

"I didn't hold you down. I was just trying to push myself up so I could see out better. I can't help it if your head got in the way."

"Mamma, tell Jackie not to do that anymore."

Tommy intervened. "Okay, guys, that's enough. We're almost to Salem and y'all are getting tired. Jackie, try not to see any more bears. Okay?"

"Yes, sir."

The trip was long, but they made it just fine, and he'd enjoyed having his new family with him. It would be crowded in Jack and Jessie's little apartment, but hopefully that arrangement wouldn't last long, and he and his bride could get their own place.

"Frankie, I don't want to waste any time. Now that we're in Salem, lets just go by the doctor's office and get our blood test."

"Honey, we just drove into town. Why don't we go get cleaned up first?"

"Nope, the office is right around the corner, so let's do it while we're this close."

A smile lifted the corners of her mouth. "Okay."

"Mamma, are we going to get married now?"

"No, Benny, we're just going to get our blood drawn, son."

"Do they use a needle? Does it hurt?"

"Yes, they do and not too much."

"Do me and Johnny have to have a blood test, too?"

"Nope, just Tommy and me."

"Good, I don't like shots."

Tommy glanced over his shoulder at the three boys in the back seat. They had been so good the whole trip he'd have to get them something special as a reward. He couldn't wait to show his family off to all of the musicians and their wives.

"Hey, after we get unloaded and get the boys settled in, lets go meet some of the guys in the band and their wives. I really want you to meet Opal, Buddy's wife, she's a sweetheart."

"From what you've told me, it sounds like I'll like her."

He drove on to the Chemawa campus and parked in front of the apartment building and honked the horn. Jack and Jessie were expecting them today, and Janie and Jody were probably looking out the window in anticipation of meeting their new cousins.

Everyone piled out of the car and he opened the trunk. "Here, Johnny, you carry this little suitcase." He handed a small bag to the reddish-blond-haired boy, then took the last of the bags himself.

Jack took one of the pieces from him and greeted him with a handshake. "How long did it take y'all to get here?"

"We left Saturday, the thirtieth and today is Wednesday, the third, so however long that is. All I know brother, is I'm getting married on November fourth, nineteen forty-eight." He felt proud as they walked toward the apartment building where everyone had gathered to greet them. "Look at her, Jack, isn't she something?"

"Sure is. You're a lucky man."

"Yep, and tomorrow's the day. I'll have her in my life forever."

Jack smiled. "Well, you'd better get this day over with first and get some rest. Jessie's got sleeping arrangements already made, so she'll tell us where to put these bags."

"If Jessie doesn't mind watching the boys, I'm going to take Frankie to meet Buddy and some of the boys."

"I'm sure she won't mind, but aren't you tired?"

"Yeah, but I'm excited for everyone to know her."

Tommy tossed and turned. Hells bells, the sun was coming up and he wasn't going to get any sleep. His heart running wild could be one reason, but his mind also reeled with plans for the future. He was the luckiest man in the world.

Everyone he'd introduced Frankie to the night before fell in love with her. He knew they would, just like he did. A few family and friends were going to go to the courthouse with them. Buddy and Opal for sure would be there.

Oh well, he might as well get up. It wouldn't do any good for him to lie there another hour. He'd get his shower and get ready for the rest of the day. It was going to be the biggest day of his life.

He was grateful when everyone else got up and he had some company. Frankie looked so sweet in her little gown and robe helping Jessie with breakfast. It was still early, but the courthouse opened at eight o'clock, and he planned to be there soon after they opened the doors.

"Frankie, how long will it take you to get ready to go to the courthouse?"

"It shouldn't take me long. I took my bath last night so all I have to do is get dressed."

"Well, let's get breakfast over with so you can go and get us a marriage license."

The courthouse was quiet except for the sound of their footsteps on the marble floor. He didn't know what to think. Even though they had their blood test and the marriage license, they were still going to have to wait three days to get married. That was the stupidest thing he'd ever heard of.

Frankie, Buddy and Opal were by his side. No one said a word. He knew they were just as disappointed as he was.

He stopped when he saw someone walking toward them. The man went into an office up the hall. "Hey, Buddy, did you see who that was?"

"Who, Tom?"

"That man that just went into that office up there."

"No, can't say I did."

"Remember that rodeo announcer that we met when we played that rodeo a few weeks ago."

"Yeah, he was a nice guy. Miller, I think his name was."

"That was him."

"So."

He couldn't stop the smile that crossed his face. "Didn't he tell us he was a judge?"

"I'll be damned, I believe he did."

Taking Frankie's hand he led the others to the man's office. When they entered, he approached the secretary's desk. "Ma'am, could I see the judge, please? Tell him it's Tommy Kizziah. I think he'll know me."

"Okay, Mr. Kizziah, I'll tell him you'd like to see him."

It wasn't long until the judge stepped out of his office. Tommy offered him a handshake. "Howdy, Judge, how are you?"

"Good, Tommy, good. What can I do for you?"

"Well, it's like this." He put his arm around Frankie. "I've been wanting to marry this woman for two years. She finally said ye,s so I went to Texas and got her. I brought her all this way, now we're told we have to wait three more days. Judge, I don't want to wait another minute."

The man nodded his head and creased his brow. "Sounds like you folks have had an ordeal, Tom."

"Yes, sir, we have."

He gestured toward the paper Frankie was holding. "Is that the marriage license?"

"Yes, sir," she said and handed it to him.

Studying the document, he smiled. "Looks like this is your lucky day, folks. Come on into my office, and let's get you married."

Tommy's heart jumped to his throat. He glanced down at Frankie and her dark eyes shone with happiness. "Are you ready, Baby?"

"Ready as I'll ever be."

Her smile warmed his whole being. "Then, let's go." He turned to his best friends, Buddy and Opal. "Are y'all ready to witness a wedding?"

"We are," Buddy replied.

"Then let's get "Er done." He followed the judge into his office, Frankie by his side.

"Step right over here." Miller pointed to a spot big enough for them all to stand. He went behind his desk. "Tommy, you and your sweetheart stand side-by-side in the middle and, Buddy, you and your wife stand on either side of them, if you would please."

Finally, his dream of marrying Frances was coming true. If only he could push the lump out of his throat and slow his heart down, he'd be doing good.

The judge took his spot in front of them. "Let's get started." He cleared his throat. "As we stand here today to bring together..."

Lost in Frankie's eyes, the words that came from the judge faded into the background. Tommy knew he would be with this woman for the rest of his life. He'd known it almost from the moment he'd met her. She had to be nervous, too. Her voice seemed weak when she repeated the words to the judge.

"Thomas Henry and Frances Patricia Kizziah, I now pronounce you man and wife. You can kiss her now, Tom."

He did just that, then the four of them left the building. "Baby, I could barely hear you say 'I do.'

That brought laughter to all of them, and he was thankful some of the tension was leaving his shoulders.

The rest of the day was pleasant as he, Buddy and Opal showed Frankie around the town of Salem. She met the rest of the musicians during the course of the day, and now it was getting late and close to bedtime. He was looking forward to making love to his bride. He'd waited a long time to hold her in his arms that way, and he wanted to make it special for her.

Unable to afford a room, Buddy and Opal had invited them to stay in their extra bedroom for the night. He appreciated their friendship. His anticipation grew when they pulled into the other couples driveway.

Buddy opened the front door of the house. "Y'all want a night cap before hitting the sack?"

Tommy grinned, glanced down at his new wife and took her hand. "I don't think so. I'm ready to call it a night."

"Okay, then. Your room is right at the top of the stairs on the right. The bathroom is just down the hall. We'll see you in the morning."

Frankie stepped toward Opal and hugged her. "Thank you so much for everything you've done. You are a special person, and I love you already."

"You're welcome, Frankie. I love you already, too."

"Buddy," Frankie said, turning toward him. "I love you, too. You are a special friend to my husband and I appreciate it."

Buddy returned her embrace. "He's a special guy Frances, and I'm glad he found a woman like you. Now, go and really make yourself Mrs. Tommy Kizziah."

"Ohhhh," She smiled, looked down at the floor and put her hand to her mouth.

It wasn't hare to tell his young wife was embarrassed. The flush in her cheeks and her reaction was a smooth giveaway. He took her hand once again. "Night, y'all, we'll see you in the morning."

"Night." Buddy said.

"Good night." Opal replied.

Frankie followed Tommy up the stairs. "Good night and thanks again," she said.

Opening the bedroom door, he closed his eyes and took a deep breath. This night with Frankie was one he'd been dreaming of for years. Now his dream was about to come true. He pushed the door open, looked down and met her gaze.

"Well, this is it, Mrs. Kizziah. We really did it."

She lifted the corners of her mouth. "We sure did."

"I guess I'd better carry you over the threshold." He bent and picked her up. She was such a little thing and light as a feather. "I love you."

She put her arms around his neck and threw her head back in laughter. "I love you, too, my husband."

He stepped through the doorway and with his foot, shut the door behind them.

Chapter 11

Spring 1950

Tommy lay in bed looking at his wife. She was the best thing that had ever happened to him. He couldn't believe he'd almost lost her. Damn booze anyway. She wanted him to continue playing music, but she also told him to stop drinking. Man, had she made a believer out of him.

His thoughts wandered back to six weeks after they were married when he played a weekend in Portland and came home drunk as drunk could be on Saturday night. All he remembered was waking up with something hitting him. No matter how he twisted, he couldn't get out of the covers.

"You SOB." Frankie had said. "I was married to one drinker, and I will not be married to another. You've done this for the last time."

What the hell was she hitting him with and why couldn't he get out of the covers? "Quiet, Baby, I'm sorry. Please."

Finally the pounding stopped and he breathed with relief. She jerked the sheet from his face and he could see what was going on.

She had wrapped him up in the bed sheet and was hitting him with his own shoe. His own shoe! "Damn, Frances, what's gotten into you?" He wrestled his way out of the sheet and sat on the side of the bed. His head spun and he thought he was going to puke. Especially when he saw the suitcase that sat on the floor beside where his wife was standing.

"Your drinking, that's what. I'm not going to stay around and let you destroy my kids' life and me. If you want to tear yourself down that's one thing. But I refuse to be part of it."

He was so sick. His stomach churned and he knew he was going to throw up. If only his head would stop spinning, he thought he'd be okay.

She grabbed her handbag. "You say you want to make something of yourself in the music business. Well, I don't think it's going to happen this way." Inhaling deeply, she picked up the suitcase.

The last thing he wanted was to lose this woman. She was everything to him. He forced down the bile in his throat and pointed to the case. "Baby, what are you doing with that?"

"I'm leaving, Tommy."

He was for sure going to lose his stomach now. He stood up, knees so weak there was no way he was going to make it to the bathroom. "Wait, wait a minute." He quickly ran past her, down the hall and barely made it before the wave of nausea made its way out. He'd never been this sick in his life. What was wrong with him?

Suddenly someone wiped his forehead with a cool rag. He could tell by the gentle touch it was Frankie. He couldn't hold his head up. Finally the wave subsided and he caught his breath. "Baby, please," he choked out. "Please don't leave. Let's talk about this. Please? I'm sorry and I love you but I'm too sick right now." He choked back another flood of sickness. "Will you take me to the hospital?"

"Tommy, you have a hangover, that's all. You'll get better."

"I'll never get better if you leave me, and right now, I need a doctor."

Man, those memories were just like it happened yesterday. He'd never felt so bad in his life. Truthfully, he did think he was going to die. Die from drinking.

He liked whisky, however, he'd always be thankful for what she'd done for him. It made him see the light. Alcohol and business didn't mix, and he wanted his music to be his business. He had barely had a drink since that day. Even though she told him she never really intended to leave, he couldn't bring himself to take the chance.

Frankie, her boys and his music were the most important things in his life, and he'd be damned if he'd let whisky ruin it for him.

He looked around the small bedroom of their new house. If it weren't for Frankie, they wouldn't have been able to buy it. She took care of all the finances and managed to save enough money to make a down payment. It wasn't a big place, but it was theirs. 818 Sunnyview, Salem Oregon.

Yep, since that Sunday morning his wife had shown him the light with his own shoe, so many things had happened. Frankie went to work at Chemawa as a housemother. All the students lived on campus and she liked the job. It was the first year for Navahos to be at Chemawa and some of them were from New Mexico, so she felt like she had something in common with them. She fit right in with the Indians on campus. After all she was a quarter Comanche herself. He wondered if that's where she got her temper.

Jessie had another baby. A boy. They named him Johnny Thomas Kizziah, after him. He was honored and the baby was almost a year old already.

Rose had gotten sick and had to stop working. Larry didn't want to run Aumsville alone so they decided to sell. Larry offered it to him and Frankie. Of course, no matter how they tried to justify buying the dance hall, they couldn't afford it after just purchasing the house. At six thousand dollars Aumsville was a great deal, but they couldn't take the chance.

Two real estate guys, Paul and Jerry, bought it and wanted to keep the band. Tommy wanted the best musicians in the area so he had been on a search for new players.

With Buddy's help, he found some good ones. They'd been really working to get the music together and today would be the last practice they'd have before starting a thirty-minute radio show on Saturday afternoons. Paul knew a local Disk Jockey, and he talked the station into doing the show. They would have to go into the radio studio, set up and play, but the sound was sure to be good.

He was proud of his accomplishments. Even though he'd quit his job at Chemawa, Frankie was still working there, but the money he made playing wasn't enough to make up for his Chemawa salary. He took a job as a custodian at South Salem High School. Hopefully, he wouldn't have to keep doing that for long. Not that he minded it, he didn't, he just wanted music to make his living.

Yes, all was well, and he couldn't wait to get to band practice.

"That sounded good y'all. Let's go through it one more time, if you don't mind." Tommy nodded to the boys in the band. Everything was coming together.

Of course, he was sorry he'd already had to replace the guys from Larry and Rose's band, but this way it would be his band. It felt natural being the bandleader, and it seemed the musicians liked and respected him. Even though some of them had only been members of the band for a short time.

"Johnny, want to count it off?"

He studied the talented folks he had and knew this was the group. They were good and they sounded great together.

Now that he'd stopped drinking, he saw how important it was to keep liquor off the bandstand. He didn't allow anyone to drink while they were working. It also helped keep him in line. If his musicians couldn't drink, it wouldn't be fair if he did.

The click of Johnny's drumsticks brought in the music. He was proud to have Johnny Reese in the band. Lawrence Welk didn't know what he lost when Johnny quit him. The short balding man had gotten tired of being on the road all the time, and Welk's band traveled a lot.

Tommy remembered the day they met. Johnny told him the story about working with Welk. There was a big difference in his music and Welk's music, but John was good and could play anything. Yes, he was lucky to have the man.

Mater of fact, he was lucky all the way around with the musicians. He glanced about the room and Evelyn's red hair glistened in the light. She could play the steel guitar as good, if not better, then any man he knew. Plus she was pretty.

He'd heard about a woman who gave steel guitar lessons. After he and Buddy went to meet her and hear her play, it was a given she would be in the band. Her husband supported her in her music, so that made things a lot easier. She fit right in and seemed like just one of the guys.

Luckily Buddy could also play bass, so he got himself a bass guitar and gave up the steel to Evelyn.

Eddy Zunck's voice rang over the microphone in rich tones as they practiced the song he'd written. He was young, the girls thought he was good looking and boy could he sing. His guitar playing wasn't too shabby either, but mostly it was his singing talent that landed the job for him.

Eddy had actually come to him for a job. He'd heard about the new band forming and wanted to be part of it. His job as a window washer made him some money, but his real love was in music. Though he'd never played dance music before, he took to it naturally and was a great asset to the group.

Tommy met his brother Jack's gaze and smiled at the sound of twin fiddles. Fiddlin' Ed Whittaker was one of the best fiddlers he had ever heard. He was married and worked for the newspaper in Salem. A pleasant man, he was anxious to audition, and once he did, there was no question he was in.

Then there was Buddy. He was a good man and could pick the strings off the stand up bass. Tommy didn't know why he didn't play bass before. It was made for him. Frankie and Opal had become great friends and every day he thanked his lucky stars for the big part Buddy Simmons played in getting this group together. He'd been in the area for a long while and knew a lot of musicians. He'd helped to find the best of the best.

Yep, this was going to be a great band and he knew what he wanted to call them, but he was going to run it by the members first. They would have to have a name before they went into the radio studio the next day to do the show.

The music stopped and Tommy took off his guitar and leaned it against his amplifier. "That was really good. Thank you all for such a good rehearsal. I know there's not any group out there that has members that are more enthusiastic about playing, and I appreciate it."

Ed Whittaker stepped forward. "Hey, Tom, we love the band just like you do." He turned toward the rest of the group. "Don't we?"

His heart swelled when they all agreed. "Good, and thank y'all. I'm glad. Hey, I've been kicking around a name for us. What do y'all think about The West Coast Ramblers?"

Almost every one agreed and whol"Heartedly liked the name. Buddy was the only one that shook his head from side to side. "No, no, that won't work."

Tommy couldn't believe his ears. "Why not? Everyone else likes it."

"I know, but I think there's something missing."

He respected Buddy's opinion. "What do you suggest then?"

"I think it should be Tommy Kizziah and his West Coast Ramblers."

He had never thought about putting his name at the front, but apparently the rest of the musicians agreed with Buddy because they were all clapping and shouting yes. Overwhelming warmth filled the room and he felt a bond with these people like he'd never felt before.

"After all, Tom, you're the one out front, the star of the show and you're going to be the one paying us." Buddy patted him on the back when everyone laughed.

"Well, that's mighty nice of y'all, so as of now, we are Tommy Kizziah and his West Coast Ramblers."

Tommy pulled his car to a stop at a red light. He was so surprised at the amount of fan mail he'd received since they started the radio show six months earlier. The Aumsville Pavilion had been packed with record numbers of people every Friday and Saturday night. The radio show was the best thing that could have ever happened, to both the band and the hall. But now he had a big decision to make.

There was another dance hall that wanted him and the Ramblers. The owners of the Cottonwoods in Albany, Oregon, approached him the day before. The Cottonwoods was bigger and they offered him more money. He would still be able to do the radio show, and a bigger hall would get him even more exposure.

The Aumsville was doing great and the change probably wouldn't make a difference. Paul and Jerry had been good to him and the band. He didn't want to do anything to hurt their business, but he had to think of the welfare of himself and the group, too.

After talking to Frankie about it, he thought his decision was final, but he refused to make the change before talking to the musicians. Their lives would be affected, too.

The light turned green and he stepped on the gas. This meeting would tell the tale. Would they go to the Cottonwoods or stay at Aumsville?

He turned into the parking lot of the coffee shop. It looked like all of the band members were already there. Good, he wanted to get the decision made so he could let Paul know what was going on.

Inside, he pulled his chair out and sat down. The waitress came up to him, pen in hand.

"What would you like?"

"I'll have a glass of milk, sweet thing." He heard the snickers from his friends.

Buddy said. "You and your milk, Tom. You stopped drinking beer and whisky and started on milk."

He smiled. "It's the strongest thing I can handle anymore."

"Yeah, since Frankie got hold of you."

Laughter came from around the table. "I knew I shouldn't

have told y'all about that." He didn't mind their lighthearted ribbing about his butt whooping. He'd deserved every bruise he got from it.

Ed Whittaker took a sip of coffee. "What's this meeting about, Tommy?"

"Well Ed-erd, they want us to play at the Cottonwoods in Albany. The owner called me yesterday to see if we are interested."

"Just for a couple of weeks or what?" Evelyn asked.

"No, they want us every weekend, and they're offering more money. That in itself is good, but it's also a bigger hall. We can get a bigger crowd and more people will hear us."

Eddy Zunck messed with the unused silverware on the table. "What about the radio show. We get lots of listeners from that."

"Yeah, we do," Tommy replied. "We'll still be able to do the radio show. I talked to the station about it this morning."

He had always known the camaraderie of this group and there wouldn't be any bickering while the discussion was going on. He sat back and listened while everyone gave him their opinion on what they thought was best. When everyone finished, he made his decision.

"I guess we'll be moving to the Cottonwoods then. I'll talk to Paul and Jerry today and tell them we'll be leaving in a couple of weeks. That should give them plenty of time to find another band."

* * *

Tommy glanced around at the band. The move to the Cottonwoods was a good one. It was just hard to believe they'd already been playing there for almost a year, but this was a special Saturday night in September. Tennessee Ernie Ford would be on stage with them.

It was the first time they'd gotten to back up someone who had a well-known name in the business. He'd had complete confidence that the band could handle anything Ford threw at them. That confidence was proven to be right at rehearsal that afternoon. He'd never been so proud of the West Coast Ramblers.

He studied the crowd as they came through the door. All of the tables were filled up, and now the benches were beginning to get full.

Every dance hall had benches that lined the walls and tables around the dance floor. If you were lucky enough to get there early, you could get a table. Otherwise, you'd have to sit on the hard benches.

With Tennessee Ernie there, the tables filled early.

"Tommy."

He recognized the deep voice behind him. "Yeah, Ernie," he replied, and turned to face him.

"I just want to tell you that you have one of the best bands I've ever had the pleasure of working with. You guys really have it together. And you sing really good. Your voice is so powerful. I hope you go somewhere, buddy."

"Why, thank ya' Ernie. I'm awfully proud of the West Coast Ramblers." He gestured toward the crowd that had gathered. "Looks like we're going to have a full house tonight. You really brought them in."

"Yeah, how about that."

"Say, Ernie, do you know Smiley Burnett?"

"Sure I know Smiley. He's a funny guy. Can make you laugh even if you're in a bad mood."

"He's going to be in town next week promoting his new movie and I thought I'd have him on the radio show Saturday afternoon."

"I think that's a great idea. It won't do either of y'all any harm, that's for sure."

"I think I'll see what I can do. Thanks, Ernie, for helping me make that decision. We'll be kicking "Er off here in about five minutes. Four songs in, we'll bring you on."

"I'll be ready."

* * *

"Hey, Smiley, how ya doin?" Tommy offered the shorter man a handshake. "I'm Tommy Kizziah."

Smiley looked up and met Tommy's gaze. "I'm fine, thanks. Man, you're one tall drink of water. How tall are you anyway?"

He laughed at the comment. "Six foot four is all."

"Damn, that's long in my books."

"Well, I can see the world pretty good from up here. Speaking of that, I see it's about time for us to go on. Are you ready?"

"Just point the way."

He walked down the hallway to the studio where the show would be. "Here we are." Smiley Burnett followed him into the small room. The band wouldn't be there that day just the two of them, and a disk jockey to help host the show. He had his flat top guitar and that's what he'd play while he sang. Mostly this show was for Burnett.

When the thirty-minute show was over, he placed his guitar back into its case. "That was great, Smiley."

"No, you were great Long Tom. I appreciate you letting me have your air time."

"Why, you're mighty welcome." He smiled and shook his head. "Long Tom. I'll have to get used to that."

"I thought it was appropriate. That's why I called you that on the air. You just look like a Long Tom Kizziah."

"I'm sure folks will be calling me that, too. However, it's kind of catchy. I think I like it."

"Good. Long Tom you are, then."

He bid his new friend farewell and went home to get ready to play at the Cottonwoods that night. Long Tom kept gnawing at him. He couldn't get it out of his mind. He walked in the door and Frankie met him with a kiss.

"How'd the show go, Long Tom?" She smiled at him.

"You were listening?"

"Of course, I always listen."

"They made me an acetate of the show today, so I'll have a copy of it forever. Only thing is it plays from the center out. But at least I have it." He put the 78 recording on the table. "What do you think about that nickname business?"

"I like it. It fits."

He shook his head. "Yeah, it does I guess." He got his guitar out of the case and sat on the couch. Long Tom. What was it that was in his head that wanted to come out? He plucked at the strings. Suddenly the notes seemed to fall from his fingertips and the tune rang through the air.

Frankie entered the room with a wide grin on her face. "What song is that? I've never heard it before."

"That's because I just wrote it."

"It's catchy and makes you want to dance. Sounds like a boogie-woogie type tune. What are you going to call it?"

"I think you just helped me with the name. How does Long Tom Boogie sound?"

She smiled. "I like it."

That evening at the Cottonwoods told him what folks really thought about his new nickname and his new song. All of the musicians really liked the tune and learned it quickly. The fans that frequented the hall all called him Long Tom and so did the pickers.

He was mostly pleased that Long Tom Boogie was a hit with the crowd. It had been requested two times after they played it originally and that was a good sign. He could only dream that someday he'd get a recording deal and that might be his first hit. Even though he didn't sing on it, his name would still be out there.

* * *

Summer 1952

"Damnit, I can't believe Archie would do that!" Tommy paced the length of the living room. "Right when I'm talking about a record deal with Four Star, this has to happen. All I wanted to do was make my musicians and me more money and The Division Street Corral is the place for us to do it. Plus, we'll get a better crowd because it's bigger then the Cottonwoods. What the hell possessed him to go to the musician's union and tell them I tried to undercut him when I didn't?"

Frankie put a calming hand on his arm. "I know that Tommy, but he doesn't want to lose his job at Division Street. He's been there for years. You can't blame him for that, but lying about how you got the job was wrong.

"I'm not the one who approached the Division Street owners. Why Mrs. Ceciliani came right up to me on the band stand at the Cottonwoods and offered me the job." He inhaled deeply and slowly blew the breath out his mouth. "I'm so damn mad right now I can't see straight."

"I know it, but it will all work out. It always does. Just wait for the hearing."

"And the hearing, that's another thing. Why do we have to wait so long for that? The son's-o-bitches have banned us from playing music in Oregon until the hearing is over."

How could this all be happening? All he wanted was to play music and feed his family. Now the world seemed to be crashing down on his dreams. Four Star was really interested in putting him on record. It was like a dream come true. "This is a nightmare. I guess I'd better get a lawyer."

"Honey, like I said, it will all work out. Now, I've got to get ready for class. Johnny and Benny are with Jessie, so you don't have to worry about them today."

He sat down on the couch. He was still working at the High School and Frankie had started a new job as a nurse's aid at Salem Memorial Hospital and had started classes to get her nursing license. That was one positive thing that was happening in their life.

And what about Evelyn having to quit? Now he would have to look for another steel player.

"Tommy, it will be okay."

Her voice brought him out of his thoughts. "I don't know if this will. With us being banned from playing in this state, the guys at Cottonwoods have already replaced us, and the other band is supposed to start this week, and I have to find a steel player. If we get to play, that is."

The shrill ring of the telephone pierced his eardrums. "Will you get that, please? I don't feel like talking to anyone."

Frankie answered the call. "Hello. Yes, this is Tommy Kizziah's house. Yes. Okay, can you hold on for a moment? I'll see if I can find him." Frankie covered the mouthpiece and attempted to hand him the phone.

He shook his head and whispered, "I said I don't want to talk to anyone."

"You'll want to talk to this man. He's the owner of Wagon Wheel Park and he heard about your dilemma and wants y'all to play there for the next few weeks."

It was hard to lift the furrow he knew his brow must be in, but he felt a smile crease his lips. "Well, hells bells, you might be right, baby. It may all work out anyway." He took the receiver from her. "Hello, this is Tommy."

"Hey, Tommy, Earl here from Wagon Wheel Park in Washington. Charlie from the Corral called me and told me what happened. He wants you to play there bad, but asked if I could help you guys out for the next few weeks. It just so happens I have an opening. You interested?"

"You bet we are. That's kind of a long drive, but I think we can handle it. Of course, I'll have to talk to the rest of the fellows before I say yes for sure. What does it pay?" He listened as the man offered them a generous amount of money. "That sounds fair."

"Plus there's another good thing about this, Long Tom. They want your show to be live on Saturday night, straight from the bandstand. It will be broadcast nationally right after the Grand Ole Opry."

The Grand Ole Opry? Man oh man, he couldn't pass it up. He knew the band members would be excited to do live shows right off the stage. "Earl, you just sold me. We'll do it."

* * *

Summer 1953

Tommy didn't know what it would do to the sound of the band to lose Evelyn, but when a new steel player, Skip Montee, auditioned for the job, he knew the music was going to be even better then before.

Tonight the crowd was good, the band sounded good and Tommy was proud to be on national radio. He was also glad he was there.

The hospital was one place he didn't like to be, but he'd had a bout of pneumonia that landed him there and tonight was his first night back. His heart soared at the response of the crowd at his return.

(This is a true life transcript of the actual radio show audio, taped in 1953.)

He stepped up to the microphone. *"We'd like to let you know, before we do this next tune, that the program"S being brought to you from the bandstand of The Wagon Wheel Park. Located on highway 30 between Camas and Washougal Washington, where you're always welcome.*

Now, our next guest is going to do you a song. He picks it and sings it almost by himself. Ah, Willie, are you ready to sing Dark Moon?"

"Ready as I'll ever be."

"Go right ahead and sing it pretty, will ya?"

Willie approached the microphone, strummed his catgut stringed guitar and as the band joined in, he began to sing. *"Dark Moon, a way up high up in the sky, oh tell me why, oh tell me why you've lost your splendor. Dark Moon…"*

When the music ended Tommy again took his place. *"Thank you very much Willie Nelson, that was mighty pretty."*

Tommy Kizziah

SQUARE DANCES
FOLK DANCES
FALL OPENING
CELEBRATION
It's All FREE!
It's All FUN
It's Another SEARS
Exclusive Feature
Tuesday
8PM
530 North
Capitol St.
FREE DANCING AT SEARS
"LOOK, MOTHER,
JUST LIKE OLD
TIMES AND I
BET THE YOUNG-
STERS WILL HAVE
A BARREL OF
FUN, TOO!"
SPECIAL .. Free
WOMEN'S STYLE SHOW
SPECIAL .. Free
FREE!
HITCHING
POSTS
REFRESHMENTS
THE BOY SCOUTS
SEARS

FALL OPENING
CELEBRATION
It's All FREE!
It's All FUN
SEARS
ROEBUCK AND CO.
SPECIAL .. Free
Tommy Kezziah and his West Coast
Wranglers will furnish the music. 7-piece
orchestra. Folk dancing, square danc-
jng. Come one, come all! Have fun!

TOMMY KIZZIAH

THE STAR THAT TWINKLED
BUT NEVER GOT TO SHINE

LONG TOM KIZZIAH   *4 Star Recording Artist*   *Featuring* HIS WEST COAST RAMBLERS

Buddy Simmons, Ed Whittaker, Tommy, Johnny Reese,
Glenn Smith & Evelyn Martin

Evelyn, Jack, Tommy, Johnny, Ed W., Ed Z., Buddy

Johnny Reese

Ray (Skipper) Montee
played steel guitar with
WCR for three years

Ed W., Ed Z., Tommy, Evelyn, Johnny, & Jack

Unknown, Unknown, Johnny, Tommy, Jack, Unknown & Unknown

Unknown, Tommy, Johnny, Unknown, Jack, Unknown & Unknown

Evelyn, Jack, Tommy, Johnny, Ed W., Ed Z., Buddy

4 STAR RECORD COMPANY INC.

305 SOUTH FAIR OAKS AVENUE
PASADENA 1, CALIFORNIA

April 10, 1951

Tommy Kizziah
1384 Waller Street
Salem, Oregon

Dear Tommy:

Thank you very much for your letter of April 6th and we are very happy to learn that "LONE TOM BOOGIE" is proving to be a good seller.

Per your request, we will press up 300 copies more and ship them to you at 1384 Waller Street. We had to order more labels so it will probably take about ten days to get this next shipment to you.

We talked on the phone with B.G. the other day and she said she was handling your records. She is a grand person and a live wire operator.

We have not mailed your record out as yet to stations in Texas as we want to find out how this record is going to go in your own territory. Have you had any more response on "LOOK UP SACRED NATIONS"?

We tried to get the best quality possible from the tape that was submitted to us. We used the same studio and the same material and process on your record that we use on our other artists.

We will be glad to review any other songs you care to submit. Since Mr. McCall is out of town for several weeks, there may be some delay in reviewing tape that you send in at the present time.

We would like to suggest that you do everything possible to get friends and acquaintances to write to the radio stations in Oregon and Washington requesting that your records be played as this will assist greatly in publicizing your numbers.

Best wishes.

Yours very truly,

4 STAR RECORD COMPANY, INC.

Don F. Pierce
Sales Manager

4 Star Record Company
305 SOUTH FAIROAKS AVENUE
PASADENA 1, CALIFORNIA

Tommy Kizziah
1384 Waller Street
Salem, Oregon

Jack Kizziah, Tommy Kizziah & Ed Whittaker

Chapter 12

Fall 1953

The heels of his and Tommy's shoes clicked on the courthouse floor. Buddy Simmons' heart pounded in his ears. Tom took such long strides, he felt like he was running to keep up. He'd never seen his friend this angry.

Tommy's Fists were clinched. "Those dirty bastards. Why didn't they tell me the hearing was today? They're trying to pull something."

Buddy knew Tommy's blood was boiling and he was fixing to get them into a heck of a mess. He had to try to talk some sense into him. "There has to be a good reason. Maybe they couldn't get in touch with you."

"Bull crap, Buddy. My lawyer knows where to find me at all times."

Tommy was in a blind fury and apparently couldn't see the numbers on the rooms of the old building. Buddy stopped in front of a closed door. Should he tell Tommy he'd gone by it or should he just let him keep walking. No, he'd better tell him or he'd get his own butt kicked. "This is it, Tom."

The tall man turned around and with a few long strides was back in front of the door he'd passed. He stepped up and turned the knob.

Buddy knew by Tommy's reaction the door was locked. He couldn't believe it. No, maybe he just hadn't turned hard enough. "What's wrong?" Buddy asked.

He tried again. "The damn thing's locked." The wrap of his knuckles against the door echoed through the empty hallway. "It's Tommy Kizziah. Open up."

There was no answer, but Buddy knew they were in there. He could hear them talking. Tommy wiggled the knob again and shook the door.

"I said let me in. I'm Tommy Kizziah and this hearing's about me. I deserve to be in there.

"Stand back, Buddy. There are men in there deciding my fate as a musician in the state of Oregon, and I'm not being allowed to be there? I don't think so." He took a step backward.

"What are you going to do, Tom?"

"I'm goin' in."

"But…" Buddy's heart sank to his toes when his friend lifted his long leg and with the force of an angry bull, kicked the door in. If they weren't thrown in jail before this was over, he'd be surprised.

Tommy couldn't believe he'd just destroyed a door in the Marion County Courthouse, but to hell with it. He wanted to know what was going on and now he'd find out. He just hoped Buddy didn't have a heart attack on him.

He glanced around the big table in the middle of the room. The looks on the men's faces were priceless to him. He walked over and stood beside the one he recognized to be from the local union. "As I said, I'm Tommy Kizziah. I think this hearing is about me. Why wasn't I told about it?"

A man at the side of the table stood. "Why, you can't just barge in here and…"

"I think I just did. Now, sit down." The man plopped back into his seat. Tommy knew if he wasn't so mad, he could have laughed about the situation, but this was serious business. There wasn't a sound in the room. He studied the face of all of the five men around the table.

"Which one of you is the judge?"

The man at the head of the table spoke, "I am."

He walked over to him and extended his hand. "I'm Tommy Kizziah, Sir. I'm sorry about all this, but I felt I had a right to be here. It's my career that's at stake, and Archie Smith told a lot of lies about me. I just wanted to make sure my side was heard."

The judge stood and accepted his handshake. "I agree, Mr. Kizziah. The bad news is you're a little late. The hearing is over. It was a closed hearing and neither party involved was able to attend. That's why I thought it best you didn't know the date. Just so nothing like this would happen." He glanced toward the door. "I can see clearly you found out about it."

Tommy felt as if all the blood ran out of his face and into his stomach. He was too late, and he's made an ass of himself kicking down the door. That was going to cost him. What was he thinking? And what was he going to do if he didn't get to play anymore?

"However," the man continued, "The good news is you were cleared of all charges. I've even called the President of the National Musician's Union, Doc. Sevrenson, and told him of the decision."

What? Good news? He looked at Buddy and a big grin stretched across the shorter man's chubby cheeks. "Did you hear that, friend? I'm cleared."

"Sure did, Tom. That's wonderful."

He turned his attention back to the Judge. "I don't know how to thank you, Judge. How'd I get cleared?"

"Well, Mr. Kizziah, there were too many witnesses that told me the truth about how you got the job at Division Street. Mrs. Ceciliani was the first to come to your defense. She told me the whole story and so did numerous others. She testified that she went to the Cottonwoods to listen to you and the West Coast Ramblers and she approached you when you came off the stage. You never went to her at all and offered to play for less money than Mr. Smith. In fact, she said she offered you more than he is getting. You're free to play in Oregon again, Tommy."

"Thank you, Judge. I knew for sure that man was going to ruin my reputation."

"I think you came out of it unharmed. Unfortunately, it took awhile because everything has to be investigated no matter how clear cut a case may seem. You know the law, and it's better to be safe than sorry in cases like this. Now, Charlie and Mrs. Ceciliani are in a room down the hall. Maybe you should go make arrangements to start playing at the Division Street Coral."

"Thanks again." He turned and started to leave the room. The reality of kicking down the door actually hit him and he stopped and stared at the mess he'd made.

"Yes, Tom," the judge said. "Now...about that door."

December 1953

Today was the day Tommy was to have his second batch of promotional pictures made for The Four Star Recording Company. He'd officially had a contract with them for a while now. Frankie couldn't have been more proud of the man she loved. He was doing so well and would have his fourth record out soon.

It seemed his dream was coming true and for an added bonus, Tommy and The West Coast Ramblers had been chosen one of the top five bands in the nation. She couldn't wait to read him the article in the Cowboy Songs Magazine. And she was really excited that he and the West Coast Ramblers would be backing Marty Robbins at the Division Street Coral on the next weekend.

She knew the other wives were thrilled about Marty, too. They would all get to go and meet him in person. There were certain perks about being the wife of a popular musician, and she was going to take advantage of every one of them.

When Opal Simmons called to find out what she was going to wear for the show, they giggled like a couple of little schoolgirls. Marty Robbins, wow.

Frankie took the new shirt off of the ironing board. "Okay, Tommy, here's this one." She handed him the pretty plaid western shirt she'd bought him especially for this occasion. He looked so nice in his neatly creased slacks and his fresh white T-shirt.

"Hey, I have a surprise for you." She pulled out the newest issue of Cowboy Songs and opened it to the page that had the picture of him and the band on it. "Look here."

He took the green covered book. "What's this?"

She couldn't contain her smile. "You and the Ramblers have been chosen as one of the top five bands in the nation. See?" she pointed at their picture.

"Well, how's about that!"

The warmth of his lips penetrated her cheek when he gave her a love peck. She loved him so much. "Want me to read it to you?"

Handing the book back to her, he said, "Please?" then sat on the sofa.

"Lefty's on the cover, Tommy. Isn't he supposed to be here again soon?"

"I think in a couple of months."

"We'll have to show this to him. Anyway," She cleared her throat. "This is the article on you guys."

(Actual Article.)
"Tommy Kizziah was born in 1915 at Rockwood, Tennessee. At the age of 12, he won an amateur contest in Oklahoma City, and following this success, he was starred over Radio Station KFJF, Oklahoma City. When Jimmy Rogers appeared with Tommy, he named him "Sonny Rogers' because of their similar styles. Under that name, Tommy appeared on Radio Station WKY and traveled throughout the

south. In 1948, he married and moved to the Northwest.

"There he assumed his real name and organized his "West Coast Ramblers' dance band. Tommy's work in Oregon was responsible for awakening public interest in Western music and entertainment. He is now under contract with 4-Star Records, for whom he waxed "Long Tom Boogie," backed with "She Just Stood Around," and "Rambler's Boogie," backed with Pretty Little Girl." His latest record is "Sleepy Little Red Head," while to be released soon is "I'm Cryin' My Heart Out For You," backed with "Two Timin' Kind." When Smiley Burnette appeared as a guest star with Tommy, he dubbed him "Long Tom," inasmuch as Tommy is 6'4" tall. Consequently, this was the reason "Long Tom Boogie" was so entitled. For the last few years, Tommy has appeared twice weekly over Station KSLM, Salem, Oregon.

She put down the magazine to help Tommy button the shirt she'd just pressed. "What do you think about the article?"

"Some of this isn't exactly accurate, but it's still really good. What do you think, Baby?"

Her fingers tingled when she touched his strong chest. "I think you're the best looking Four Star Recording Artist ever. These new shirts are going to really look nice in your pictures." His smile melted her, just like it always did. She was so lucky to have him for a husband.

She wanted to tell him the other news she had, but now wasn't the time.

"Thanks, Baby. You're the best looking wife of a Four Star Recording Artist, too. And I liked the article. Can't wait to tell the band."

She watched him tuck his shirt in. Even though he was thin, he had a muscular build. All of the women wanted to go with him, but she kept her eye on him pretty good. If he tried to step out of line, she'd know about it. However, she didn't think he ever would.

It was too bad his pictures wouldn't be back in time to give one to Marty, but there would be plenty of time for that. She just knew her husband was going to be a Country Western star. Even if he weren't, she'd love him anyway.

Tommy got the phone call from the photographer that his promo pictures were in. He couldn't wait to see them. When he got the first ones, everyone, especially the teachers at South Salem, wanted his autograph. Having never had an education, he couldn't write too well, so he practiced his signature. He was getting pretty damned good at it now, if he did say so himself.

"Morning Tommy," the lady behind the desk said. "Here after the pictures of you and the ones of the band, too?"

"Yes, ma'am."

She pointed to some boxes in the corner. "There they are. They turned out really nice. Want to see them?"

Of course he did, but... "Well, not right now. I want my wife and me to see them together the first time."

"Oh, that's sweet. Well, you can just take them with you if you want."

He heaved one of the boxes into his arms. It was heavier than he expected. "Will you get the door for me, little lady."

Excitement surged through his veins as he placed the boxes of photos in the back seat of the car. Was his dream coming true? Could it really be happening to him? Was he on his way to stardom? The contract with 4-Star, Fifth rated band in the Nation, radio broadcasts akin to the Grand Ole Opry? And backing guest stars like Johnny Cash, Marty Robbins, Ray Price and Lefty? Maybe he'd be as big as they were someday and could stop being a custodian. However, it was a good income with benefits.

When he pulled in the driveway of the house, he realized he didn't even remember driving home. His mind was reeling with ideas and dreams. He couldn't wait to call the members of the band to share the photos and the magazine article with them.

"Oh, Tommy, these are great!" Frankie stood at the kitchen table and took each pose out one at a time. "Look at you so handsome with your foot propped up and your guitar resting on your knee. You look like the professional that you are. And look here at the bottom of it in big black letters. Long Tom Kizziah, 4 Star Recording Artist featuring His West Coast Ramblers."

"Look at this one of the band and me. It turned out really good, too."

"I think they're all just wonderful. I'm so proud of you."

He knew she was proud and he hoped he could live up to her expectations. She was a special lady, and he was glad to have her. All of the band's bookkeeping, payroll and taxes was left up to her. If it weren't for Frankie, he didn't know what he'd do. She was the rock he'd always needed in his life.

He pulled her into his arms. "Come here and give me a kiss, wife."

They held the kiss for a long while and when he pulled back and gazed into her eyes, she had a glow about her and a big smile on her face. He continued to hold her in his arms. Her warmth was a security for him.

"Tommy," she glanced downward, but still grinned, "I have something to tell you. Something really important." She broke his grasp, turned and stepped away. "Oh, never mind, it can wait.

What was wrong with her? He grabbed her arm and gently pulled her back into his embrace. "Oh, no you don't. Now you've got me curious. What is it?"

"Are you sure you want to know?"

He lifted her chin, forced her to meet his gaze then raised one eyebrow. "Frances," he playfully scolded.

"Oh, all right." She took a deep breath. "I'm going to have a baby."

"Ah"Ah..." Wait a minute. What did she just say? A wha—
"A what?"

"A baby."

He swallowed the lump in his throat and tried to slow his heartbeat. "A real baby?"

She pushed away from him and laughed. "No, you big lug, a toy baby. Of course a real baby!"

Everything was happening so fast. He'd better sit down while he could still pull the chair away from the table. The room spun, but Frankie's steady hand on his shoulder helped him settle down. "A baby," he whispered

His wife sat in his lap. "A baby, she confirmed."

He straightened his furrowed brow and wondered if his smile went from ear to ear like it felt it did. "A baby!" He stood up and nearly dumped Frankie on the floor. "Oh, I'm sorry. Are you all right? Do you need to sit down? Can I get you anything? What should I do?"

"First you need to settle down. I'm fine. There's nothing wrong with me. I'm just pregnant."

"You sure you're okay?"

"I'm sure."

Lifting her small frame into the air, he spun her around. "Oh, baby, this is the best day of my life. We're going to have a baby."

June 1954

The baby could get here any time and it was Saturday night. Tommy was on his way to pick up Buddy and Eddy Whittaker. They were going to ride with him to Division Street tonight.

All the guys had helped him, Frankie and the boys move into the new house they'd bought on Norwood Street. It was much bigger than the one on Sunny View and had a full basement, too.

He thought about some of the great memories he had of

the little two-story house on the other side of town and had to laugh. Frankie's boys were a hoot. One time he heard water or something coming out of the boys' bedroom window upstairs. He glanced out the downstairs window to see what they were doing. Hells bells, they were peeing out the window. They confessed they'd done it a lot of times.

Then there was the time the boys were jumping on an old bedspring in the back of the house, and Benny landed the wrong way and got a crick in his neck. He'd never forget the conversation between Benny and Frankie that day or the tears in the little one's eyes when he sobbed and asked, "Mommy do you think it's broke?"

He laughed out loud at the memories. He loved those little fellers. However, right now he had to wonder if the folks driving next to him thought he was a crazy man. Sitting alone in the car laughing.

Life was good. His records were being played on the radio and the band sounded better than ever and the baby would be here soon. He hoped it was a boy, but if it was a girl, he'd probably love her just the same.

The only thing that wasn't going good in his life right now was the owner of 4 Star. The man put up a good front, but deep down inside, he thought the guy was a jerk. He also wondered when any money was going to start coming in from the recordings. He'd been told they were selling well, but there wasn't anything at 4 Star to back that up.

If something didn't happen soon, he was going to think about changing labels.

Stopping in front of Buddy's house, he honked the horn. Opal waved at him from the doorway and their boys, Donnie and Larry, shyly stood by her side as she kissed her husband goodbye. Opal and Frankie got along well and she had really helped Frankie through this pregnancy.

"Hi, Tom."

"Hey, Buddy, you ready for tonight?"

"Yep."

"Good. I think Willie Nelson's going to come up again tonight and be our guest."

"You mean that disk jockey from Washington?"

"Yeah."

"He's a nice guy isn't he, Tom?"

"He is, and he's married to an Indian woman. They've got a couple of kids, and he was a talented songwriter, too. I've heard some of his stuff. His timing with the beat of the music is a little off, but you can't argue that the man has a style all his own."

"Can't argue that for sure."

The drive to pick up Ed was short and they reached the Corral in record time. Willie was waiting by the stage when they arrived.

His sandy brown hair was combed neatly straight back and the shorter man reached to shake Tommy's hand.

"Hey, Tommy, how ya' doin'?"

He returned the shake, put his guitar case on the stage and flipped the hinge's open. "Good, Willie, glad to have you here."

"It's good to be here, too. Hey, can I talk to you some time this evening?"

Tommy wondered what was on the man's mind. He'd never sounded this serious about talking before. "Yeah, Willie. Let me get set up and ready to play and I'll come join you at a table."

All he had to do was tune, check to make sure his amplifier was working right and he was done. He went to the table where Willie was and took a seat. "What's up?"

Willie sat back in his chair. "Tom, do you still have that trailer you used to haul your equipment from one place to another?"

"Yeah."

"Well, I'm thinking about moving to Nashville. I hear

that's where the music scene is really going on. Would you consider selling that trailer to me so I can move my family?

I've got a trunk full of songs and somebody needs to hear "Em."

"I'd consider that, Willie. I don't think we're going to be playing anywhere but here at The Division Street for a long while. I won't need it. When are you planning on leaving?"

"All we gotta do is pack up, Tom. How much do you think you want for it?

"It's not the greatest trailer in the world, how about fifty dollars?"

"Sold. Can I pick it up next week?"

"That"Ll be great. Now lets get to entertainin' these people, what do you say?"

"Okay." Willie smiled and they both stood. "And, Tom?"

"Yeah?"

"I won't forget you when I'm rollin' in the dough."

He hoped the guy made it, but it was a hard row to hoe and he wasn't sure Willie had it in him. "Good luck. Call if you need anything."

Chapter 13

July 2, 1954

Frankie glanced at the bedside table. Five o'clock a.m. Her contractions had wakened her a little earlier, and as she watched the clock, they were getting closer together. This one was harder than the last two.

Her pregnancy had gone pretty uneventfully, although her morning sickness was worse with this one then either of the other two. When it was all over, she'd be relieved. It had been ten years since she had Benny and she wasn't getting any younger. The doctor thought her delivery date would be earlier. She knew it wouldn't and tried to tell everyone, but no one believed her.

She smiled at the thought of Tommy calling every Saturday night between sets to find out if she was okay or having pains. He would have left the band high and dry if she went into labor while they were playing.

Her husband had gotten a kick out of teasing her throughout her pregnancy about the baby being red-headed. Since Johnny and Benny's dad was red-headed and Johnny was strawberry blond. He thought it was a funny joke.

What she thought is that it would really be funny if the baby did have red hair. Then the last laugh would be on Tommy. Thinking of her boys, she was glad they had spent the night at Jack and Jessie's. That would be one less step they would have to do today.

Another pain. This one was stronger. She would have to wake

Tommy soon, but she wanted to put it off as long as possible because she knew he would run around like a chicken with it's head cut off once he was up.

Sometimes he and the band booked outside Division Street and special functions around the area. This weekend would be one of those occasions. She was just thankful last night was Wednesday and he was home. If she'd waited until this evening to go into labor, he would have been gone to play at the Rodeo in Molalla.

She took a deep breath and tried to time her contraction. The pain was too intense. "Oh, oh me...Tommy?" She pushed on her sleeping husband's shoulder. "Tommy."

"Hmm, huh?"

"I think it's time to go to the hospital. The baby's coming." Frankie held her stomach. "I've been putting it off, and watching the clock, but I can't put it off any longer. My contractions are getting closer together. We'd better go."

She'd never seen him move that fast. He was out of the bed and had his trousers on before she could even sit up. It made her happy to see him so excited.

She made her way to the bathroom and turned on the light. The next thing she knew, Tommy was standing in the doorway with her suitcase in his hand. "Tommy, you're already ready to go?"

"Sure, we'd better hurry."

"Well, Honey, I have to get ready first. I can't go like this."

He gestured toward the case. "I'm going to put this in the car. I'll be right back."

She brushed her teeth and combed her hair. Another contraction. This baby was going to come faster then the others. She'd better get a move on.

She stepped into the bedroom to put her cloths on. Tommy came back in and looked frantic.

"Aren't you ready yet?"

"I'm hurrying as fast as I can."

"I've called Dr. Trailstead. He's going to meet us there."

"You already called him? For goodness sakes, I may not be ready for awhile." Another contraction. She took a few deep breaths and it finally passed. "I'll hurry."

Tommy was glad Frankie was finally ready to go. It had taken her almost three hours from the time she woke him up. He took a calming breath. This was it. He was going to be a father. He felt like he was Johnny and Benny's father, but he wanted a child that had his name, his blood.

He loved those boys like they were his own and couldn't imagine loving a child more than he did them, but they had another dad and he would never be able to take the man's place. Even if the boys didn't get to see their real father much, he was still their real father. No matter how much he loved them, they would always be Red Jones' sons.

A grin tugged at his lips. Maybe now they'd have a new little brother to play with. He hoped so anyway.

"Tommy!"

Hells bells, what was he doing? Now he was the one stalling. He'd better get his butt in gear.

He gave Frankie his watch so she could time her contractions on the way to the hospital. The pains were getting closer and closer. They pulled into the hospital lot and rushed in.

"Ma'am," he said to the nurse at the admission desk. "Ma'am," his voice louder this time.

The lady looked up. "Yes, what can I help you with?"

He gestured toward Frankie. "My wife's having a baby."

Frankie clutched her stomach. "Oh, and Honey, it's coming fast."

"Oh, my goodness. Let me get you a wheelchair." The nurse left and returned moments later. "Here you go. Sit right down there, we'll get this paper work done and get you back to the OB ward."

He didn't like seeing the woman he loved in such pain.

Actually, he felt guilty for getting her pregnant. However, he was excited, too. Soon he would be holding a baby in his arms and it would be theirs. Frankie had been giving the nurse their information, but her frantic cry took his attention.

"We'd better hurry! This baby isn't going to wait much longer."

"How long have you been in labor Mrs. Kizziah?"

"About four hours."

"Oh, baby's don't come that fast. I'm sure we have plenty of time. We just have a little more to do here, then I'll take you back."

The short time at the nurse's desk seemed like a week to him, but finally they got her back to labor and delivery.

"Mr. Kizziah, you may as well go and get some breakfast or something. It's going to be awhile until she has this baby, and we have to prep her for the procedure."

He took his wife's hand. "How are you feeling, Mamma?"

"I feel like this baby's going to come faster than they think, but I guess they know what they're talking about. You go ahead and go. I'll be fine."

He didn't want to leave, but if they weren't going to let him stay with her, he'd go crazy just sitting around waiting. He glanced at the clock. "Okay, it's nine o'clock. I'll be back in a couple of hours."

"That will be fine. I'll see you later."

After brushing her lips lightly with his, he left the small room and said a silent prayer that his wife and baby would both be okay.

He went to tell some of his friends and his brothers about the baby coming. He'd been gone less then two hours but now, as he walked down the hall toward the labor and delivery wing, he wasn't sure he should have left at all.

Two nurses rushed up the hallway pushing a gurney. He hoped that wasn't Frankie, but his gut told him it was and when they got closer, his fears were confirmed. His heart plummeted into his stomach, and his breath caught in his throat.

He fell into step with them. "What's wrong?"

"Mr. Kizziah, you're about to become a father."

The lump in his throat went down hard. He looked down at his wife. She looked groggy, but when he met her gaze, she still had a smile for him. "I-I thought you said it was going to be a few hours."

"We were wrong, now if you'll excuse us, we have to hurry, the baby's trying to come out already and we need to get her to the operating room. You'll have to go into the waiting room now."

They turned the corner and blasted through some double doors, leaving him right where he stood.

He found his way to the waiting room. It seemed like he looked at the sterile-looking clock on the wall every hour, but it was every minute. Time was at a standstill, at least for him and he couldn't seem to sit down.

Finally the door opened and a white clad lady stepped inside. He glanced at the clock one last time and it read eleven thirty.

"Mr. Kizziah?"

"Yes,"

"You're the proud father of a baby girl."

A girl? A girl? "It was a girl?"

"That's right. She'll be in the nursery in just a few minutes and you can look at her through the window."

His heart fluttered. He didn't think there had ever been a moment in his life he'd been more proud than he was right now. "It's a girl."

The nurse grinned. "Yes, sir, I know."

"Frankie. How's Frankie."

"Well, Mr. Kizziah, she's bleeding a lot."

Forcing himself to take a breath he asked, "Is she going to be okay?" What would he do if something happened to her? He couldn't live without her.

"The doctor's sure he can get the hemorrhaging stopped, but it may be awhile before she gets into recovery."

"But she will recover, right?" The calming smile that crossed the woman's face seemed to soothe his anxiety.

"Your wife is going to be fine, Mr. Kizziah. Don't you worry. All you need to think about is getting to see you're little girl." She turned toward the door. "Follow me. I'll show you to the nursery."

He walked behind her through one corridor and then turned into another. Looking ahead of them, he saw a large framed window. The woman stopped at a door just before they reached glass.

"I'm going to go into the nursery. You can look through that window right there and see all of the babies. I'll point yours out to you."

He took a few steps and gazed through the casement. The nurse didn't have to point out his daughter to him. He knew exactly which baby she was. She had lots of black hair and was as pretty as a picture.

The woman picked her up and held her close to the pane. His heart pounded in his chest and tears welled in his eyes. He'd never seen anything so tiny be so beautiful. Never had he felt so much love for such a small little thing. He had to see Frankie and thank her for giving him such a gift.

He watched as the nurse placed the baby back in her bed then turned to go and check on his wife.

An hour passed before someone came to tell him he could see her. When he walked into the room, his loving wife looked like she'd been through hell. He guessed she had.

The hospital bed was only a few steps across the room. Frankie's big brown eyes opened and she looked at him. "How are you, Mamma?" Her voice was weak and his heart went out to her.

"Oh, I've been so sick from the anesthesia. And I've lost a lot of blood, but I'm better now. Have you seen her?"

Frankie's hand was cold when he picked it up. "Yes, I've seen her." Just the thought of her made his heart skip. "Mamma, I could have picked her out if she'd been in a barrel with fifty babies. She has lots of black hair and is the most beautiful little thing I've ever laid my eyes on.

The corners of her lips lifted into a smile. "Your face is sure lit up."

"Why not? You've just brought a ray of sunshine into our lives, and I love you for it." He placed her hand to his lips. The love he felt inside right then was indescribable.

"My little baby girl, Mary Frances."

She furrowed her brow. "Now, Tommy, we've already discussed names. It's a girl, so her name is going to be Sharon. Sharon Patricia Kizziah."

He loved getting her dander up and as happy as he was right now, they could name her Jim and he wouldn't care. "Ah, Baby, any name's fine with me. I'm just glad she doesn't have red hair, that's all." Dodging her playful slap, he couldn't stop the laughter that billowed from his chest.

Summer 1955

Tears fell from Frankie's eyes. Tommy hated to see her heart broken, but there was nothing he could do about it. Benny and Johnny had decided to go back to New Mexico and live with their paternal grandparents, Mommy and Pa Jones.

The boys were eleven and thirteen years old now, and had made many train trips back and forth form Oregon to New Mexico, almost every year since '49'. They couldn't make up their minds which place they wanted to live, so they had the best of both worlds. One year here, the other, there.

However, Benny had grown tired of the trips and had decided this would be his last. He wanted to live in Lovington from now on. They didn't know exactly why he'd made that choice, and as much as she wanted to, Frankie didn't question it. She just hoped it would be like all the other times and he would want to come back in a year.

Tommy shifted Sharon to his other hip. Frankie felt like Benny knew what he wanted. No matter how much it killed her inside, she was going to let him go. He, however, didn't agree. He thought Benny should be right where he was. His grades were good, and he seemed happy. The truth be known, he would really miss the boy, and Johnny maybe even more. Both boys held a special place in his heart. Hopefully, they would get homesick and come back.

It tore him apart to see Frankie like this. She always made sure they would be safe on their journey. Either she would travel with them or someone else in the family or a good friend would go.

This time it was Frankie's sister Tootsie. She had come to visit and had to make the trip back anyway. It worked perfect for the boys.

Tootsie was the oldest of Frankie's siblings and a very colorful person. It was hard to believe they were kin at all, knowing how grounded Frankie was and how adventurous Tootsie was. Hells bells, the woman was an airplane pilot, and if she'd owned a plane, she would have flown herself out there.

Frankie sniffed and wiped a few of the million tears she'd shed from her cheeks. "I'm going to miss you two so much. Now, if you need anything, anything at all, you just call us. Or if you want to come home, you call."

"We will, Mom, stop crying. I'll write you a letter as soon as I get there." Johnny wiped a tear from his own eye.

"No, you call me. I want to know the minute you get to Mommy and Pa's." She bent, kissed his cheek and hugged him tight.

"Okay." He returned her embrace.

She turned her attention to the youngest. "Benny, you be good and mind Aunt Tootsie, you hear."

"I will, Mom, don't worry."

Every time the boys left, he could see his wife's heart breaking into little pieces. She took Benny into her arms and sobbed. Tears welled in his eyes. Damn, this got harder every time. Maybe it was because Benny had said he wasn't coming back to live. He knew that once the boys were on the train, Frankie would cry for the next few hours. She always did.

He was thankful he'd gotten out of the hospital from his last bout of pneumonia so he could be here with her. It seemed he had the stupid stuff more and more the last few years. He must have gotten his lungs from his mother. God rest her soul.

The conductor yelled, "All aboard!"

"Frances, it's time for us to go." Tootsie hugged her sister. "They're going to be fine. Don't worry." She ruffled Benny's hair. "We're going to have a good time."

Johnny stepped forward. "Yeah, Mom. Heck me and Benny have been on this train so many times, we know the porters by their first name."

That brought a little well-needed laughter. He handed the baby to his wife and gave the boys a quick bear hug. "We love you guys."

"We love y'all, too."

Frankie handed Sharon to Johnny. "Give your sister a kiss."

Tommy could tell Johnny adored his little sister. He always had a sparkle in his eye when he looked at her. On the other hand, Benny loved her, but didn't think she would ever be able to play baseball, and that was his first love.

They said their final goodbyes, and he watched Tootsie and his other two children disappear into the passenger car.

The sound of the whistle echoed through the air and the wheels started to turn. Frankie cried and waived when she saw the two little faces on the other side of a window.

"Call as soon as you get there!"

Johnny nodded his head, smiled his sweet smile, then they were gone.

Spring 1957

Tommy drew the big, commercial sized mop over the floor of the empty corridor. After all the years he'd been doing it, he had the technique down to a science and would have this floor done in no time. The South Salem High School students were gone for the day, but he still had work to do.

Never in his life would he have guessed that he'd still be pulling a mop across these floors. He'd thought by the time he was forty he would be making a living by playing music full time, but it didn't look like that was going to happen.

Now he was forty-two, time had flown by and in the last few years not much had changed. He was still playing and recording, but his carrier wasn't going anyplace.

A lot of the artists who had been on 4-Star had moved on to a different label, and he did the same for all the good it had done him.

Being a little ticked wouldn't describe the way he felt after the fact that with all of his releases through the 4-Star label, he'd gotten one check for ninety-seven cents and that was it. Why, hells bells, Patsy Cline had been with 4-star and after she left them, she won the Arthur Godfry talent show and now had a hit record with Decca called Walkin' After Midnight.

He couldn't help thinking about it and now. When it was so quiet in the school, it was the worst time for his mind to wander. It seemed he couldn't win for losing, but he'd be damned if he gave up.

Though he and the band weren't playing as much at The Division Street Corral, they were always busy and still did the Saturday Night shows with the NBC affiliate radio station KGW. Heck Harper and his band were taking up the slack, and he had even gotten himself a television show out of Portland. Maybe if he'd had an education he would have been able to do more, but he doubted it.

One of the biggest problems was that none of the guys in the band wanted to go on the road. They all had good daytime jobs and families and didn't want to take the chance of losing any of it. However, in this business, you had to take chances in order to get anywhere.

Frankie supported him in his music as long as he could do it locally, but she would never let him quit his job at South Salem to go gallivanting around with no real assurance it would do any good. He guessed he didn't really blame any of them. If it were meant to be, it would have been.

Right now it looked like he would be doing his live radio shows from the Division Street Corral as long as they'd let him.

He had a great fan base, but mostly on the West coast. However, they did get request letters from as far away as Alaska.

At least the West Coast Ramblers had a good reputation and were still the best band around. They all loved playing behind the big stars that came in as guests, and that hadn't slowed down any. Once a month, somebody with a big name came in.

He thought of the conversation he and Frankie had that very morning before he went to work.

"Jimmy Wakely is going to be at Division Street with us next week, Mamma. I think he's got a new movie coming out."

"I know, I wish I could be there, but I'm saving my time for T-Texas Tyler. He's coming in a few weeks and Janie has already said she'd baby-sit."

The cutest little sparkle came in his wife's eyes when she spoke of Tyler. "He's your favorite, isn't he?"

"Oh, I guess. I think he's nice, that's all."

Tex was a nice guy and he came to the Corral quite often. So did Rex Allen, The Maddox Brothers and Rose, Marty Robbins, Johnny Cash, Tommy Duncan, Ferlin Husky, he could go on and on.

He remembered the first time Ferlin came to play and Frankie went to pick him up at the airport. She felt sorry for him because his boots were scuffed up and looked old. He reassured her that the man probably just wanted to be comfortable.

One of his favorite guys to come play was Faron Young. He and Faron had developed quite the friendship. They tried to stay in touch as much as possible.

His brother Jack still played with them some, but he had his own band now and was mostly playing around the area on his own. Jack's daughter Jody had gotten married in February. Jody was the prettier of Jack's two girls and Janie had a personality out of this world. He loved both of them and hoped his niece would be happy with her new husband Carl.

Brother Red and his new family had moved to Salem a few years earlier. His oldest daughter, Jean, stayed in Spur with her mother Essie May after she and Red divorced.

Red remarried in nineteen forty-four. He and his second wife, Dealva, had four daughters. Frances Darlene, Edith Arlene, Katrina Marlene and Margaret Sharlene. There were only five years difference in all the girls' ages and the youngest turned six in January. They were all as different as night and day to him.

When they'd all get together and play cards he liked it. Or, since he and Frankie had gotten their television, Jack and Red and their families would come over and they'd order Chinese food and watch the fights or something.

The corners of his mouth lifted at the thought of his oldest son. It was nice having Johnny home again, too. That boy was the closest thing to a son he'd ever have. He loved him with all his heart and was pleased he'd decided to come back to Oregon to finish school at South Salem. Frankie was as happy as she could be that at least one of her boys was with her.

The drain of the big utility sink in the cleaning room slurped as he watched the dirty water from the cleaning bucket swirl down it. After rinsing the mop, he put everything back in its place.

His heart did a little pitty-patter when he thought about going home to his family, and he realized he was happy with his life. Even if he'd never be a big star, he was a star to a lot of people including his wife and baby girl.

Being a custodian wasn't the best job in the world and he'd never be rich, but his family loved him and that was dear to his heart. Plus, he could go golfing just about any time he wanted. That was a good thing, too.

It was time to go home for the day and he couldn't wait to see his wife, son and that little black-haired girl waiting with open arms to greet him.

Tommy & Frankie's wedding picture

Tommy & Jack

Frankie, Virgie, Dealva &
baby Darlene

1950's

Tommy, Frankie & Sharon

Frankie & Sharon

Tommy & Sharon

Benny, Tommy, Sharon & Johnny

Chapter 14

Spring 1958

"Hurry, Tommy, I don't want to be late."

He put on his jacket. "We're not going to be late, Mamma."

"Make sure you've got the movie camera. I want to get this on film."

"Ever since we got that thing, you've wanted to get everything on film." She shot him a nasty glance and he smiled.

"Well, it's Saturday night. Lefty Frizell's coming to the Corral to play with y'all tonight and it's his thirty first birthday. What's not to film?"

Everyone, including himself, had been excited to find out it was Lefty's birthday. The man had been at the Corral many times before, but tonight was going to be special. The wives of the musicians had cooked up a surprise birthday party for him.

"Okay, I'll get the camera. Is Janie Bell here yet to baby sit?"

"She's here."

He grabbed his cowboy hat. "Then I'm ready if you are."

When they pulled in the parking lot of the dance hall, the crowd was gathering. Lefty was one of the people's favorites. It looked as if the Zunck's and the Simmons' were there already, and Lefty would be there any minute. He got out of the car and Frankie followed.

Once inside, he watched the three wives find a table that was big enough to seat them and all their husbands when they came off for a break. At the end of the long table, they left a place for

Lefty. Most of the time the band members didn't sit down during breaks, they had other things to do like mingling with the crowd, but maybe tonight would be different.

When the rest of the musicians got there, Tommy led the way to the stage so they could get tuned up. Everything was just as they'd left it the night before.

The neon sign on the back of the stage that read, Tommy Kizziah and his West Coast Ramblers, was on in all of its brightness. He wondered if the movie camera would pick it up clearly.

Hopefully, Frankie would get some good pictures of them tonight. He'd like to have them so when he wasn't able to play music anymore, he could at least watch them and remember what it was like.

He came off the stage and turned toward a commotion at the door. Poor Lefty was trying to get inside, but a bunch of women were waiting for the opportunity to meet him.

He made his way over to the group of girls and laughed. "Okay, ladies, let the man through." He approached his friend. "Hey, Lefty, how are ya?"

Lefty extended his hand. "Good, Long Tom, you?"

"Good. Happy Birthday." He returned the shake, then led the younger man to the front of the stage where some of the musicians and their wives were gathered.

"Damn, thirty one, I'm over the hill." Lefty saw that Frankie had a movie camera. "But, I dressed for the occasion." He opened his long coat and twisted and turned so she could get the effect of its beauty on film.

Tommy went around to watch as Lefty posed for the camera. "Now that's a mighty nice blue western suit, Lefty. With all that sparklin' stuff and those white fringes, you're right in style."

"Ain't I though?"

Deloris Zunck was quite the flirt in Tommy's eyes. She was a cute young thing and liked to flaunt her beauty, but always in a playful way. At least he hoped that's what she was doing, for

Ed's sake. He watched when she approached Lefty then stood by with a smile as the scene being played for the eight-millimeter camera. This was going to be good.

Mrs. Zunck put her arms around the guest star and gave him a hug, then her husband, Eddy, came up with fisted hands and acted like he was going to pummel Frizell. He couldn't believe Lefty went along with the gag and played his part.

That would be some good stuff to watch later, and some really funny memories. He glanced at his watch. It was almost time to start the show so he went up on the bandstand. It was going to be a good night.

* * *

"I'm sorry, Tom, but I have to quit."

Tommy hated to see his fiddle player go after all those years. "Well, Ed, I'm sorry, too, but I understand. I never expected you and Lucy to divorce."

"I didn't either. It wasn't her fault. I'm to blame for everything. You know that."

"Yeah, I guess I do, Ed." He did know. Lucy couldn't put up with Ed's infidelities. He was a good man. He just liked other women. It was a shame, too. They had those two beautiful little girls. Hells bells, Susan and Sharon were the same age. The two were so close they used to suck on each other's bottles.

"I hope you can find someone else to take my place."

"Oh, I'll find someone, but they won't be you, that's for sure."

"We've been good friends over the years, Tom. I hope we can stay friends."

"There's no doubt about it. We'll be friends forever. What are you going to do?"

"I think I'll go to Reno. I've always wanted to live in Nevada, so now's a good time to make the move. Lucy and the girls are going to stay here. I'll be back and fourth to see my kids."

"Anytime you come back into town, you give me a call. Come out and sit in with us at the Corral."

"I'll do that, Tom." He stood. "Will you tell Frances bye for me?"

"I'll tell her." He hugged the man he'd known for nine years. "You have a safe trip, my friend. We'll miss you."

Ed returned his embrace. "I'll miss you guys, too."

There were tears in Ed's eyes when he turned to leave. He blinked back his own tears and watched as Ed Whittaker drove away. Damn, he was a good man. Why did he have to do what he'd done? He didn't understand.

He hated it when they lost musicians; they were all his friends. Buddy, Ed Zunck, Johnny Reese and Ed Whittaker had been with him from the beginning. Man oh man, he hoped this wouldn't cause the break up of the entire band. What would he do without them all? No, he wasn't going to allow himself to think that way. Everything would work out.

Right now he had to go. He and Frankie had hired a Nanny to take care of Sharon and the woman was to arrive soon. How would it be with someone else living in the house? He'd never thought about a nanny, but this lady seemed perfect. Thank God they could afford her.

Now that Frankie had finished nursing school, she was going to work at the mental hospital, Fairview Homes, and he worked all day at the high school. With Johnny in school all day there was no one to watch Sharon. Frankie decided it was time she had more help. He agreed. She worked her tail off all the time. Keeping the house, going to nursing school, working and keeping up with a four year old who was a handful.

Four years old. Damn, time flew by. He'd gotten a phone call a couple of months back that Mary's daughter Mary Lou had her second child. Mary Lou was still a kid herself in his eyes. When he thought about her, he remembered that little ten-year-old girl standing beside his sister when he went to visit years ago. He didn't want to admit it, but he was getting older. And so was

Frankie, and she didn't need to be doing all the work around the house.

He tried to do everything he could to help, but it seemed like he was always doing something with the band. Why, hells bells, he'd just rented a bunch of recording equipment and set it up in the basement. All the guys came over, and they put down a few songs on reel to reel. Maybe someday they could transfer them to records. He realized how thankful he was that Ed Whittaker had stayed long enough to finish the recordings.

Getting out of the car at home, he saw the the nanny, Nettie Sours' vehicle. He knew it was the right thing to do. Frankie had already made the decision to hire her and that was okay with him. He trusted his wife's judgment one hundred percent.

Summer 1959

"I just love this place. This is it, Tommy. This is the house I want to buy."

That was a good thing to hear. It seemed like they'd looked at a hundred houses in the last couple of weeks. If this was the one Frankie wanted, this was the one they were going to get.

He couldn't believe they were already looking for another house after selling the house on Norwood and buying one on High Street only a year earlier. He had always liked the house on Norwood, and they both loved their next-door neighbors, Don and Mable Quinn.

They had become good friends over the years and The Quinn's little boy, Chuck, was Sharon's favorite playmate. She called him Chucky, and had missed him ever since they moved to High Street.

Jessie and Jack lived about a block from the old house on Norwood. Frankie missed Jessie. The women would have their hen sessions and drink their coffee. He and Frankie wished now that they'd never sold that house and moved, but hindsight was always clearer.

He glanced around the large empty room of the house they

looked at now. Pleased she'd found something she liked. She was never crazy about the High Street house, but Red's wife, Dealva, loved it, so his brother bought it.

This house would be closer to Frankie's sister, Bobby. Don, Bobby and their three children had moved to Salem early that year. They were the first of his wife's kin to come to the area. She seemed happy to have them there.

He liked Don and they played golf together when it was possible. Golf was a sport he'd taken up a few years earlier and he loved it. Matter of fact, he wished he were on the course right then.

"Tommy, are you listening to me?" Her voice broke into his thoughts.

"Huh? What did you say?" He noted the disgusted look on her face.

"I said, isn't this den big?"

He realized he'd been following her around not paying a bit of attention to his surroundings. Talk about being lost in thought.

"Yeah, it's big all right."

"Oh, I really like it, but do you think we need something this big now that Johnny's graduated and is going to leave for the Air Force soon?"

"I think if it's what you want and it's something we can afford, then let's get it."

Her smile lit up the whole room, big as it was, and his heart melted. Even if he hadn't liked it, he would let her get it, because it made her happy.

"You've talked me into it, Tommy."

He followed her to the front of the house where the real estate man waited.

"We'll take it," she boasted.

January 1960

Tommy turned into the drive of their new home on Judson. Frankie hadn't stopped crying since they'd left the airport. He cried, too, when Johnny waved to them from the top of the stairway leading into the airplane that was going to take him to Germany for his tour of duty.

The boy was now a man and was on his way to a life of his own, and Tommy couldn't have been more proud. "Frances, Johnny's going to be all right. He'll be home before you know it."

She held a tissue to her eyes. "Two years. He's going to be over seas for two years."

God, seeing her like this ripped at his heart. He turned off the ignition and pulled her to him in hopes he could calm her sobs. "Mamma, he's been gone to New Mexico for two years before and he always comes back."

She sniffed and leaned into his embrace. "I know, but I always knew I could get on a train and go to see him and Benny if I wanted or needed to. I can't go to Germany."

Her small frame shook with each tear shed. "I know, I know." What else could he say? It was true, she couldn't go to Germany, but she could go to see Benny. "Hey, I have an idea. Why don't you go to New Mexico and see your family and Benny? Maybe you need your mamma right now and they all live right there in Lovington."

She sat up and attempted to stifle her tears. "Do you think that would be okay? I mean, I haven't been home in a few years, and I would love to see everyone. It won't make me miss Johnny any less, but it might make it easier."

"Okay, you start making arrangements. Now, I'm going in the house. It's cold in this car." He pulled the handle, opened the door and began to get out.

"Tommy."

He turned toward his wife. Her eyes were red and swollen but she managed a grin.

"Thank you, and I love you."

"I love you, too, Mamma." He didn't know when or why he started calling her mamma, but she was the mother of their children, so he guessed it was appropriate. Even if it wasn't, it was his affectionate name for her, and he'd call her that till the day he died. To hell with what other people might think.

Summer 1961

Tommy looked at his wife sitting in the chair next to his hospital bed. "How in the hell can one person have pneumonia so many times? I've had this stuff about every year for the last few years."

"Oh, Tommy, don't cuss. I know you've been sick a lot with respiratory problems, but the doctors will find out what's causing it sooner or later."

"Well, I hope it's sooner than later. I want to be alive when they find out."

Frankie stood and walked to the bedside. "It does seem like you're worse every time you get it now days. You were so delirious with fever it scared me."

"I'm sorry, I didn't mean to scare you."

"You couldn't help it, you were sick. You didn't even know who I was or where you were. Whatever it takes, we have to do something to stop this from happening so often."

It was true. He was worse every time. It scared him, too. It took longer and longer to recover every time and the band had a hard time finding someone to replace him when he was gone.

They had started accepting fewer playing jobs in the last few months. It seemed everyone was losing interest. When they weren't playing on the weekends, some of the musicians played with other groups.

He didn't like it when one of the band members couldn't be there when the West Coast Ramblers had a gig, because it was hard for him to get anyone to sit in that was good enough. At least good enough in his eyes, so he knew what it was like when they had to get someone to sit in for him.

A deep cough racked his lungs and the burn and sting went down to his toes. Definitely, something was going to have to be done about this.

October 1962

Tommy forced himself to speak. "Frankie, something's wrong!" he stared at the blood in the toilet where he'd just thrown up.

Frankie ran down the hall. "What is it, Tommy?"

"I'm puking up blood."

"Oh, my gosh! I'll call Dr. Trailsted and get something for you to throw up in on the way to the hospital. I bet your ulcer is bleeding and that's dangerous."

His heart was going to beat right out of his chest. He'd had stomach problems for a few years now and tried to drink a lot of milk. That seemed to make it better. Apparently, it didn't. The last thing he wanted was to be back in the hospital, but this was something that needed attention now.

He swallowed hard and tried to slow his breathing. He didn't feel sick right now, so he'd better get ready to go.

Frankie was already packing him a bag when he entered the bedroom. She took such good care of him.

"The doctor said not to waste any time getting to the hospital. He wants to run some tests, but he thinks the same thing I do." She shut the lid of the case. "There, let's go."

"I'm sorry this is happening right when your family's coming to visit from Lovington."

"Don't worry about that, Tommy. That's what's wrong with your stomach right now, you worry too much."

"You probably won't be in there but a couple of days anyway. We'll be fine."

A wave of nausea went through him but he was able to fight it back. Weakness overtook him and things in the room got dim. He couldn't pass out, he couldn't. Frankie wouldn't be able to get him up and she'd have to call an ambulance. "Let me lay down for just a minute before we go."

"What's the matter? You're white as a ghost."

"I'll be okay, I just need to lay down for a minute." He inhaled deeply and lay across the bed. Shortly he began to feel like he could walk to the car. His legs wobbled beneath him.

"You must be losing a lot of blood, Tommy. We'd better hurry."

Frankie gazed out the large picture window in the living room. The wind was really blowing now. A hurricane on Columbus Day, and to think it was this far inland. That was unheard of. It would have to happen while Tommy was in the hospital and her Mom, Dad brother-in-law and sister were visiting.

She glanced at her sister, Maxine, and her adopted baby boy, Michael. Max had made a pallet on the floor in front of the fireplace for the one-year-old. Her dad, Isom, and sister's husband, Cotton, had gone out to cut some firewood.

The weatherman said the storm was going to get a lot worse before it got better. They'd made a trip to the store earlier. Almost all of the flashlight batteries were gone and people were jerking survival kits off the shelves as fast as they could. Canned goods and non-perishables were going quickly, too. Surely this wasn't going to be that bad, but everyone had to be prepared for the worst.

She'd just feel more secure if Tommy were home, but his bleeding ulcer was a bad one, and Dr. Trailsted wanted to keep him in the hospital for a few days. He'd already called numerous times giving her instructions. Put food in the basement, get plenty of wood and put some water in containers. She closed the drapes and stepped back when she realized the other thing he'd told her was to keep everyone away from the picture window.

"Mommy, can I play with Michael?" Sharon asked.

She brushed one of the little black curls from her daughter's face. "Yes, but be gentle with him."

"Can he play catch?"

"If you roll it on the floor to him, he may be able to play a little bit."

"Can he color?"

"No, I'm afraid he'd eat the crayons."

"Well, what can he do?"

Cotton and her father came in the back door both carrying an armload of wood. "Why don't you go and help Granddad and uncle Cotton. Hold the door open for them, and if they drop anything, you can pick it up for them. You can play with Michael later." Sharon's dark brown eyes lit up.

"Okay." She turned and ran to the back door.

* * *

The wind whipped and raindrops pelted the windows of the hospital room. The hurricane was at its peek, and the rain had been coming down for a couple of hours. In just the last few minutes, the staff rushed around and the lights flashed off and on frequently. What was going on out there?

Tommy was feeling much better, and they'd gotten the bleeding stopped in his stomach. He didn't know why they were keeping him there. He needed to be home with his family.

A nurse entered his room. "Mr. Kizziah, how are you feeling?"

There was a questioning look in her eyes and an urgency in her voice. "Fine, why?"

"The first floor is flooding and we need to get some patients that can't get around moved to different places. Would you be willing to help?"

"Damn right. Let me get my clothes on, and I'll be right there." The young lady shut the door behind her. He took off his pajamas and sat on the side of the bed to put on his trousers. Those poor people that couldn't get out of bed must be scared to death.

He'd never been through anything like this before, and he was frightened a bit, but at least he could get himself around. Putting the last button on his shirt through the hole, he walked to the door, opened it and stepped outside his room. The hallway was filled with people in hospital beds.

He found the nurse that had asked for his help. "Hey, little lady, what do y'all need me to do?"

"I think they need you on the first floor more then we do. You'll have to take the stairs."

Hells bells, did she think he was going to get in the elevator when the power was going on and off? "Where's the stairway?"

She pointed. "Down the hall, and take the first right. It's just a little way down."

He nodded and took his leave. A lump formed in his throat as he passed the folks in the beds in the hallway. This was a bad situation, and it was good to be strong enough to help, but he wished he were with Frankie and Sharon.

The devastation of the storm was worse then Tommy had imagined. Frankie told him that she and the others didn't go into the basement because the big walnut tree in the back yard was moving so much she was afraid it would fall and trap them down there.

A tree had uprooted and fallen on Bobby and Don's house. Thankfully, when the electricity went off all over town, Bobby and Don came over to Frankie's and his house. They didn't have a fireplace and everything in their house was electric. They weren't there when the tree fell in.

The stove at his house was gas so it could be used to cook and for a little heat on top of the heat from the fireplace. Frankie did a good job of taking care of things.

Even though there was a storm going on, it sounded like they had a nice family reunion. All cooped up in one house.

Now that he was home, and everyone was gone, things were getting back to normal and there was another storm brewing.

It was time to get out of the music business.

CHAPTER 15

November 1962

Tommy glanced around the room at all the musicians that he'd grown to love over the years. He knew what this discussion was going to lead to and his insides churned. He didn't want to do it, but he knew it was best for all.

He'd chosen to have the meeting at his house so everyone could be comfortable. "Well, fellas we may as well get started." Watching as his friends took a seat, he inhaled a calming breath, for as much good as it did. The sound of his heartbeat was still pounding in his ears.

"I wanted to talk to y'all about something. We haven't been playing every weekend like we used to. The band still sounds as good as it ever did, but I feel like we're losing interest in some ways. I just wanted to know what some of y'all's thoughts are on it."

Buddy Simmons cleared his throat and relaxed back into the sofa. "Tom, I'll tell you what I think. I think we've had a good thing going for us for over ten years, and it's time for something different. We're all getting older, at least I am, and I need a change.

As you know, my boys are playing now. Donny plays bass and Larry plays a hell of a good guitar, too. I'd like to put a little group together with them and get them started in the business."

Tommy knew Buddy was thinking about putting a band

together with his boys, and he thought it was a great idea. Buddy's boys were great kids, and he was glad they had a man like buddy to lead them into the music business. "Eddy Zunck, what do you think?"

"Tom, you know I love the West Coast Ramblers. Always have, but I agree with Buddy, it's time for a change. Everyone knows I've written a lot of songs and have recorded some of them. I think I would like to put more effort into promoting my songs and myself. Maybe get my own group, too."

Having heard most all of Ed's songs, Tommy agreed. "You have some damned good songs, Ed, and you're still young enough I think you can do something with yourself." He switched his attention to Johnny. "Mr. Reese, how about you?"

Johnny shook his head, glanced at the floor then met his gaze. "Tommy, I'd play with the West Coast Ramblers until the day I die, but if we're going to disband, which it sounds like this is the way it's going, then I think I'll just take the time to retire.

Tilley and I would like to do some traveling. Since I'm retired from my day job already, no weekends of playing to worry about, it will be easier for us to get out of town."

Tommy's heart was heavy in his chest. Everything he and these men had worked for all those years was going to the wayside. However, it was time to move on, no matter how much it hurt.

He went around the room to the rest of the musicians. Each one told how they felt about the disbandment, and they all agreed. It was time to quit.

"I agree with everyone. I think it's time for a change. I apologize for all the times I've been sick over the last few years. That hasn't made it any easier for any of us. I'll take care of canceling the few weekends we already have booked and I'll talk to Jim at the radio station and tell him of our decision. Heck Harper plays a lot at the Division Street now, I'm

Aumsville-1950

Tommy & Jack

Ed Whittaker

Evelyn

Opal Simmons

Ed Whittaker

WCR

Tommy Kizziah & WCR live at the Strawberry Festival in
Lebanon, OR in the early 50's

Evelyn, Jack, Tommy, Ed W., Ed Z., & Buddy

Evelyn, Buddy, Johnny, Tommy, Ed W., Ed Z. & Jack

Ed & Linda Whittaker

Ed W., Evelyn & Jack

Evelyn & Al Kennee

Tommy & Evelyn

Tommy, Johnny Jones, Evelyn & Ed W.

Tommy, dancers, Buddy, Ed W. & jack

Ed W., Ed Z.,Jack

Tommy & Ed Z.

Evelyn, Tommy, Johnny, Ed W., & Buddy

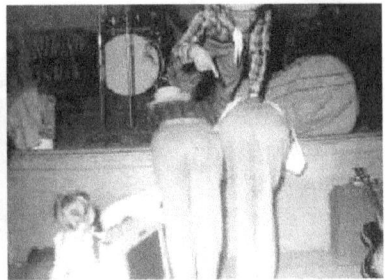

Linda Whittaker, Ed W., Ed Z., & Tommy

Evelyn, Jack, Tommy, Ed W., Ed Z., & Buddy

GUEST STARS

Rex Allen

DUNCAN, featured with
Duncan and his Western All-Stars

Glenn Duncan

Tommy Duncan

TOMMY DUNCAN
and his WESTERN ALL-STARS

TOMMY DUNCAN
and "BING"

Joe "Fingers" Car

Blackie Crawford

DIVISION ST. CORRAL

Lefty Frizzell

Tommy Kizziah, Lefty and Ed Zunck
Live at Division St. Corral

228 Ferlin was inducted to the Missouri Country Music Hall of Fame May 2005
He remembered Tommy & WCR and obliged Sharon with this autograph

Ferlin Husky

Ann Jones

Ray Price & Tommy

Ray Price

Wade Ray

MADDOX BROS. AND ROSE

MADDOX BROS. AND ROSE

MADDOX BROS. and ROSE

"T" Texas Tyler

Rosie & Rita

The Sneed Family

B WILLS

BOB WILLS
and his TEXAS PLAYBOYS

BOB WILLS
and his TEXAS PLAYBOYS

Jimmy Wakely

Billy Jack Wills

FARON YOUNG

FARON YOUNG

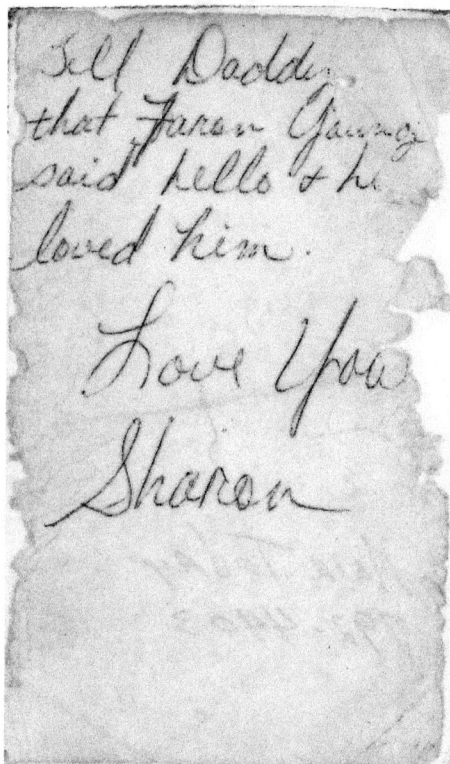

Tell Daddy
that Faron Young
said hello & he
loved him.

Love You

Sharon

In 1976 I moved to Lubbock Texas and went to barber school. I played with the Larry Triter band at the Red Raider Inn. Faron Young was a guest star with us in 1977, and told me what good friends he and my dad were.

Before he left that night he asked me to tell Dad he loved him. This ia a copy of the note I wrote to my mother so she could relay the message since Dad couldn't read.

Dad carried it in his wallet from that day until he died in 1989. I laminated it and now carry it in my wallet.

Sharon Kizziah-Holmes

sure if they want to keep the show going, he'll be glad to take it over.

I love the hell out of all of you guys, and I'm sorry it has to end. However, I think it will be good for all of us."

He fought back the tear that threatened to spill onto his cheek. "I have to say one more thing. It may be over but..." he smiled at the memories that flooded his mind. "We've had a hell of a good time over the years, haven't we?"

Sitting back in his chair, a kind of peace washed over him when the men voiced their agreement. Over the next couple of hours his emotions peaked and plummeted as they talked about old times. The memories flooded back of things he'd forgotten and he realized how blessed he'd been to know these men. Man, how much he enjoyed the music they made over the years.

How many lives had they touched with their music in all that time? He'd watched many big stars come and go over the years, and he felt like their equal, even though he and the West Coast Ramblers never made it big nationwide. They were better than some and worse than others, and God must not have intended for him to go any further in this business than he did, so he wouldn't question it. This chapter of his life was over.

Summer 1963

"My baby boy is getting married." Frankie put the snacks she'd made for the trip in the floorboard of the car. "I can't wait to meet his girlfriend."

"You'll be able to do that in about three days." Tommy placed the last of the suitcases in the trunk. "Do you have the overnight bag and the small bag you packed for the road?"

"Yes, they're right here." She gave them to him.

"I'll put them in last so they'll be easy to get to."

"Where's Sharon?"

"I'm right here, Mommy."

She was amazed that Sharon always woke up in a good

mood no matter what time of night or day it was. She was a good child, but she was stubborn and a lot of times when she didn't get her way, she'd have a tantrum.

Tommy couldn't find it in his heart to spank his little girl, but she wouldn't hesitate to get a switch and give her a little sting on the legs. Thankfully, she didn't have to do that very often.

"Hi, baby girl. We're all ready to go. I've made you a bed in the back seat so you can go back to sleep if you want."

"Thanks, but I think I'll stay up and bug you guys."

That wouldn't last very long. Every time they got in the car, Sharon would go to sleep. However, they hadn't made this long trip by car in a long time. She and Sharon had gone on the train once a few years back. She slept a lot then, too.

"Whatever you say."

The last stretch of road was the one between Tatum and Lovington. It was only twenty miles but it seemed to take forever. Finally, she could see the Lovington water tower.

Benny would be getting married the day after tomorrow. She couldn't wait to see him and meet, Patsy. The rehearsal dinner would be where she would meet the bride to be's family for the first time.

What would the girl's folks think of her and Benny's dad being divorced? Looking over at Tommy's handsome face as he concentrated on the road, she didn't care. He was such a good man and Den, the boys' real dad? Well, he was just Den. He'd remarried a lady named Leona and was living in Hobbs.

It broke her heart when Johnny got out of the service and decided to move to Hobbs. He still lived with Den and Leona.

Johnny had told her he had a nice girlfriend. She was sure she'd meet her while they were there, too.

* * *

The brown grass blew in the wind as they pulled into

town. Her boys were grown. It seemed like yesterday they were little tots clinging to her leg. Time went by too fast.

Reaching over the back seat she shook Sharon's shoulder. "Baby girl, it's time to wake up. We're here."

Sharon sat up in the seat and glanced out the window. "I don't remember it being this flat. And brown, why is it so brown?"

She and Tommy met each other's gaze and she chuckled when she saw the amusement in his eyes. "They need rain I guess."

"Humph, they need trees, too."

Laughter bubbled up this time and she welcomed it as they all joined in.

Benny looked so handsome standing at the Alter. The way he cocked his head to the side told Frankie he was in his shy mode.

He had a great sense of humor, but down deep inside, he was shy. His little wife was a doll, and she'd fallen in love with her when they met.

Her heart fluttered when Benny took the ring and placed it on Patsy's finger. His words were barely audible, but she knew what they were and couldn't stop the tears from flowing. No matter how hard she tried, they wouldn't stop.

He looked so sweet standing there. Patsy was at least a foot shorter then he. They reminded her of she and Tommy and the difference in their height. If they loved each other as much as she and her husband, they'd be together a lifetime.

Johnny brought his girlfriend to the wedding and she was beautiful. Her name was Pat, too. Now, they had four Patricia's in the family, Sharon, Pat, Patsy and her. Well, Pat wasn't in the family yet, but she bet the pretty young lady would be before long.

She wiped a tear from her cheek. The one thing she wanted most was to move back to Lovington and be with her family. It would probably be better for Tommy, too. His asthma had given him such problems lately, and something was causing all that pneumonia.

This wasn't the time to think of that. Her heart soared with pride when her son kissed his bride. It was done. They were married, and she was one of the happiest women on earth that she got to witness it.

May 1964

Tommy was going to miss all of his friends at South Salem High School, and he was especially going to miss his brothers, Jack and Red. They had become close again after the Ramblers broke up.

He stacked another packed box atop some others. The trees and green grass were a couple of the things he'd miss the most. Never in his wildest dreams did he think he'd move back to the high plains, but they'd be leaving for New Mexico on the fifteenth and that was that.

Frankie entered the room. "Hi, Honey. You're getting a lot done. How do you feel? Are you breathing okay?"

"I'm feeling pretty good right now. Whoever heard of someone being allergic to mold?"

She smiled. "I'm sure there are a lot of folks who have allergies to it, and you're one of them. The doctor said that's why you've had pneumonia so many times in the last few years."

"Mamma, I know that's what he said. That's why we're moving to a warm dry place. I just hate leaving the Oregon beauty for brown grass and mesquite bushes."

She began to put some more things in a box. "I know you don't like it in Lovington, but Johnny's back there now living with Den and his wife Leona. That's one good thing, and another is that some of my family's there, too. I'll get to be with Mamma and Daddy in their last years."

"I was thinking, I might be able to put a band together

there and just play a little around the area."

"That sounds like a good idea. We'll be within a hundred miles of a lot of bigger towns. Lubbock, Midland, Odessa, Roswell. There's a bunch of places you could probably play. I'm sure Hobbs has some night clubs, too."

At least that gave him some hope of not being bored to tears in a town of less then five thousand. Even though the West Coast Ramblers had broken up a couple of years back, he had still played around with some of the guys and Jack. He guessed he's never really stop playing. He could just see himself now walking with a cane and playing for an old folks dance.

It was too bad Sharon didn't inherit his singing talent. He'd tried a few times to get her to sing and she couldn't hold a tune. Granted she was only nine, but, hells bells, when he was nine he had his own guitar and was teaching himself to play. Apparently she got her vocal chords from her mother's side of the family.

However, he knew that there had to be some musical ability in that family because Johnny could play guitar and sing. He remembered the many times the boy had set up his amplifier and played along with the Ramblers when they were practicing or playing somewhere. He wondered why Johnny didn't pursue it harder. He seemed to like it.

Of course, the young man could have gotten his musical inclinations from the Jones', too. Oh, well, it didn't matter to him. At least one of his kids played and sang a little.

"There," Frankie said. "That's the last of the boxes. All we have left is the personal stuff we'll need on the road."

He'd always been a proud man and there was something bothering him. "Frankie, are you sure Joe and Gerry don't mind if we stay at their place? It's been so many years since we haven't owned our own house, I feel uncomfortable about barging in on your brother and his wife."

"We won't be there long. We'll find a house to buy. Heck,

we'll probably get moved in before school starts back. Besides, we won't be staying in the house with them. They have a small trailer house in the lot behind their place that we're going to live in until we can find something."

He'd been so poor when he was younger and had to depend on others to house him, he just hated going back to it now, even if it wasn't for the same reason. "I know all that, really, but I want to find something soon after we get there."

"We will. I'm sure of it."

Nettie Sours walked into the room. "I've got all of my stuff in my son Bob's car and I'm ready to go."

He met the gaze of the older woman he'd grown to love over the years she'd lived with them and taken care of Sharon. "Well, granny, we're really going to miss you. Wish you could go with us."

Frankie walked over and hugged her. "Yes, we wish you could go."

Tears came to Nettie's eyes and spilled onto her cheeks. "I wish I could go, too. You kids are like family to me, but my real family is here and I have to stay."

Approaching the two women, his heart broke. They were leaving, they were really leaving this place he loved so much, and with his illness he'd never be able to move back. This would be his last move. Hells bells, he was fifty now and too old to be moving all over the country.

"Granny," he said, "I'm going to miss our nightly pinochle games after dinner."

She looked up at him, smiled and touched his face. "You just remember how many times I won."

A laugh made its way out his mouth. She was so cute. "No, you remember how many times I won. You know I was always the champion."

Getting a tissue out of her purse she shook her head. "Oh, Tommy Kizziah, you story teller, you'll never change." She wiped her nose and glanced at Frankie. "Honey, I don't know how you put up with him, but take care of him anyway."

"I will, Granny, I promise."

Sharon ran into the room. "Granny Sours! I thought you were gone. I love you."

He cleared his throat and fought back his own tears now. When his little girl hurt, he did to. This move wasn't an easy one, but one they had to make.

* * *

Tommy passed the papers to Frankie to sign. They would be able to move into their new house that weekend and he was glad. It was a small but nice, two bedroom, brick house. The only thing he didn't like about it was the pink bathtub, toilet and sink in the bathroom, but he'd learn to live with it.

The banker took the signed documents from Frankie. "Congratulations Mr. and Mrs. Kizziah and welcome to Lovington."

"Thank you. We're glad to finally get a home." She placed the ink pen on the desk. "We've been here for six weeks and have been living on my brother Joe's property in a trailer they have behind their house. It was nice of him to let us do that, but it's not like having your own place."

"No ma'am, it's not," he replied, studying the paper work. "According to these, you've both already gotten good jobs here."

"Yes, sir. I'm a nurse and I went to work at Lea General hospital on the Obstetrics floor. I've never delivered babies before, but I've found I love the work. I'm used to a bigger hospital, but this one is much more personal, and I like the people I work with."

"Mr. Kizziah, how about you? I see you're working for the school system. Are you a teacher?"

Was he a teacher? Hell no, he couldn't even read. "I'm a janitor."

"Oh, I see."

He saw the chiding look on his wife's face. He didn't mean to be so harsh and really hadn't realized the bitterness he felt over this move. "It's a stable job. Working for the school has good benefits and I'm grateful for that."

It wasn't this man's fault he had allergies to the mold that grew in, Oregon, that he quit the music business or that he had to move to this God forsaken country.

"Well, that's good. We're glad to have you in our community."

"My son went to school at Lovington High School. He got married last year and is going to college at ENMU in Portales."

"Oh, really? What's his name?"

"Benny Jones."

"Of course, I know Benny. He's quite the baseball player."

"Yes, he is, he wants to be a coach someday."

"He'd be perfect for it. Who'd he marry?"

The sparkle in his wife's eyes was evident when she talked about her children. "A young lady named Patsy Clingo."

He smiled. "The Clingo's are really nice folks. They've been customers of our bank for years. I'd say he's probably got a good one."

"We think so. Our son Johnny's going to get married soon, too. His girl's name is Pat Rhea. Do you know the Rhea's?"

"Yes, I do. This town's so small I think everyone knows everyone. Jim"S a disc jockey out at KLEA, isn't he?"

"He sure is."

"That Pat is a beauty and a good girl, too."

Tommy knew if he didn't get his lovely wife out of the office, she'd talk about her family all afternoon. She loved them and was proud of them so he didn't blame her, but he had other things to do besides sit around here.

He stuck his hand out to the man behind the desk. "Thank you very much for your time, but we'd better be going."

The banker stood and returned his shake. "You're wel-

1960's

TJ, Mary, Tommy, Red, Bill, Jack and Ike Kizziah

Back: Jack's kids, Janie and
Johnny Thomas
Middle: Red's girls, Marlene,
Arlene and Darlene
Front: Red's girls Sharlene and
Tommy's girl Sharon

Bill at Lon Kizziah's
grave site
DeQueen, Arkansas

Sharon 1959

Sharon, Tommy and Frankie
Christmas 1966

Tommy and Myrtle were reunited once again in the 60's. This is the family. Ivy's husband Wesley Kettler, Martha's husband Bobby Monroe, Martha (Gusp and Myrtle's daughter), Wesley and Ivy's son Randy Kettler, Myrtle, Ivy holding Martha's son Darrell, Ella Maude, Jimmy and Ella's son Rory. Unfortunately, Ella's only son Rory was killed in a car accident in his early 20's and Ivy's only son, Randy died of cancer in 2004 at the age of 49.

Darrell Monroe, Myrtle, Rory and Ella

Martha and Myrtle

Randy, Myrt and Darrell

Rory and Darrell

Tommy and Myrtle

Jimmy and Tommy

Tommy and Ella

Bill's son Byron, Mary, Mary Lou, Lou, Bill, Non-family member, Tommy, Mary and Reuben's son Terry and Mary's husband Reuben.

Bill and Tommy playing a hootenanny in Texas.

come, and if we can do anything else for you, just let us know."

"Will do."

Frankie picked her purse up and rose. "Thank you, honey, you've been very nice."

"You're welcome, Mrs. Kizziah. Give me a call if you need anything."

Tommy took her hand and led her out the door. They were starting a new life in a new town in a new house. Maybe this move wouldn't be so bad after all.

Summer 1965

Tommy trailed through the students as they readied to leave for summer vacation. He liked the kids and the staff at Taylor Junior High. It hadn't taken them very long to recognize his experience and promote him to supervisor. He was proud of that.

It had been almost a year since the move, and he found himself settling into a routine with his new job and new band.

He'd met quite a few musicians and finally put a group together. Just lately he had booked some jobs in the area. It looked like they were going to stay busy during the Christmas season playing private parties. They weren't the West Coast Ramblers, but they were good.

There were a couple of nightclubs in Hobbs, but both had house bands so he and the others would have to hire out for weekend dances. That was okay with him. Anything to start playing again.

It was great to be reunited with Johnny. He had grown up to be a good man and a hard worker. He married Pat the summer before and decided he wanted to be a New Mexico State Policeman. After attending the academy, he and Pat moved to Deming, New Mexico.

It was good to know that both boys were happy in their lives. He knew that Frankie hoped that one of them would make her a grandma soon.

Sharon was only eleven and it would be many years before she would be interested in boys. At least that's what he wanted to think. He didn't want her to ever get married. She needed to stay his little girl forever, but he knew that wouldn't happen.

However, he was glad that she had finally shown some interest in music. At the Kizziah family reunion the year before, she sang a song he didn't even know she knew. His heart swelled with pride because all of his family was there, including his father's last wife Myrtle.

It was the first time he'd seen his youngest brother, Jimmy, and his little sisters, Ivy and Ella Maud, since his trip to Brenham in forty-two.

Man, you could sure tell they were Kizziahs. It baffled him, however, that they had thought their name was Rogers all those years. They didn't find out their birth name until they were almost grown. Why Myrtle didn't tell them the truth, he didn't know, but they knew now and were proud of it.

Sharon's voice singing that song came back to mind. Maybe in a year or two he'd buy her a guitar.

Fall 1966

Tommy couldn't have been more surprised when he picked up the phone and heard Willie Nelson's voice on the other end. He'd know it anywhere.

"Hey, Tommy, how ya doin'?"

"Willie, that you?"

"Yep."

"How the hell did you find me?"

"Well, I knew you moved to New Mexico, so I just made a few phone calls and found out you're in Lovington and got your number. Are ya playin' much?"

"No, not really. I've got a little band, but nothing like the Ramblers."

"Man, it"D be hard to beat the Ramblers. Y'all were great. Best band on the West coast in my estimation."

He agreed, but that was in the past. No matter how much he wanted to, he couldn't go back. "Thanks, Willie, I appreciate it. I miss it, too, but I've moved on with my life. Matter of fact, I'm going to be granddad soon."

"The hell you say."

"Yeah, my oldest son, Johnny and his wife are having a baby in February. We're looking forward to it."

"I'll be damned."

"Enough about me. Hey, I've been hearing your songs on the radio. You're getting popular. Congratulations."

"Thanks, Tom. I'm doin' pretty good. It's keepin' me busy, that's for sure. Hey, I have a favor to ask you. I'm gonna be playin' there close to ya tonight at a place called Glen's Bar."

"Yeah, that's about fifteen miles from me."

"Well, we blew an amplifier last night and I have a mic. on the blink, too, I was wonderin' if you have some we can use."

"Sure, sure. I'll bring them out." If Willie was doing so well, why wouldn't he have an extra amplifier in case of emergencies? Oh, well, he didn't care. This would be a good opportunity to take Sharon out to meet him.

"I appreciate it, Tommy. We'll be gettin' there about six this evenin'.

"Okay, I'm going to bring my daughter with me. She sings some, and I'm trying to get her more interested in music."

"Sounds good. I'd love to meet her."

He had another idea. "Say, my daughter-in-law's daddy is a disc jockey at the little radio station here in Lovington. He does a show every morning over KLEA. If he comes out, would you give him an interview for the show?"

"Damn right. We need all the publicity we can get. Bring him with you."

"We'll see you tonight."

CHAPTER 16

Tommy went into the back room of the house where he kept his musical equipment. The room had been a carport when they moved in two years ago, but with a little help, he enclosed it to make an extra room in the small house. There was a bed, dresser and a storage area, and some of it was set up so he could play and sing back there when he wanted to practice.

Gathering his things and thinking about seeing Willie again brought back great memories. The music business had once been his life, now it was only a pastime. He wished he was where Willie was right now, but it was never going to happen. His best wishes went out to the man, and he hoped he made it big. It looked like he was on his way.

"Hey, Daddy, what are you doing? I thought you didn't have to play tonight." Sharon sat on the bed.

"I don't, but do you remember the other day when we were in the car and that guy came on the radio I told you I knew?"

"Willie Nelson?"

"Yeah, that's him. Well, he's playing out at Glen's Bar tonight. Want to go meet him?" Her eyes lit up and warmed his heart just like her mother's did when they sparkled.

"Heck, yeah. Just wait until I tell the kids at school. That"Ll be cool."

He looked at her tall lanky frame as she relaxed back on

the bed. It looked like she was going to have the tall Kizziah build. She looked like his side of the family, too, but at the same time, she favored Frankie. He knew she was going to be pretty when she grew up. "Do me a favor?"

"What?"

"Willie wants to borrow this amplifier. While I get it ready to go and put it in the car, would you call Jim Rhea and tell him Willie called and he'll give him an interview if he wants it?"

"Okay. Then I have to figure out what I'm going to wear."

Twelve years old, all girl, and he loved her more then life itself. "Thanks, Baby."

* * *

Tommy and Sharon followed Willie and Jim into a room at the back of the bar. This was the biggest nightclub in the area, and he and his band had played there a couple of times. The sound was good tonight and so was the crowd. Sharon seemed to be enjoying herself, too.

"Tommy, I really appreciate you doing all of this for me tonight."

"You're welcome, Willie."

Jim sat up the small recorder on a nearby table. "Willie, if you want to have a seat, we'll get started with the interview."

Tommy studied Willie as he took a place at the table. He had on a dark blue suit and his hair was combed high on his head with not a hair out of place. He looked like a country singer, that's for sure.

Moving the microphones to their proper places, Jim said, "Okay, Willie, you ready?"

"Yep."

"Here we go." Jim turned on the knob and the tape started.

(Actual interview)

"Well we have a great one here folks we'd like to present to you on our program this mornin'. Young Willie Nelson into this country from, ah, where in the world is it, Willie? All over?"

"Well, we've been workin' in Texas the last few days and we snuck across the line into New Mexico tonight."

"Ah, tonight we're talkin' to you out here at Glen's Bar. We're kind of back here in a little apartment here, away from the band stage and all of this. But there's a good crowd out to see a good show, and how do you like this country."

"I love it here. It's a good crowd and a very responsive crowd, too."

"Very good. They like this Country and Western music and I'm sure they certainly like your style of it. I know we certainly do around KLEA there in Lovington. We play a lot of your records and always glad to get "Em."

"I've heard a lot of comment about KLEA and, from what I can understand, you're doin' a great job for country music, and I appreciate it, and I know all the country music fans do, too.

"Well, thank ya, Willie. We're certainly glad to talk to you tonight I believe you said a little earlier you were kind of down here from out of Amarillo tonight?"

"We worked Amarillo last night and we're going into Oklahoma City tomorrow night."

"Making a big swing around over the country?"

"Ah, quite a large swing. We started out on this particular tour in Beaumont, Beaumont, Texas, and then went from Beaumont to Fort Worth, Texas and Fort Worth to Amarillo, from Amarillo to here. Then tomorrow Oklahoma City then Dallas, Wichita Falls, Houston and then somewhere else, I forgot." Laughter.

"It gets kind of difficult to keep up with the itinerary after so long of time. Do you get to where you just, ah, when some-

body points you to a door you just go through it?"

"I wrote a song about it. **I Take It One Day At A Time**. *And that's the only way."*

"That's real good, and speaking about your writing songs, you've written very many good ones, Willie. We certainly do like to play them. **Your Touch Me, Crazy, Funny How Time Slips Away, Hello Walls** *and, oh there are numerous of "Em. Are you still writing "Em occasionally along?"*

"I'm still writin', I guess, about the same number of songs a year as I always did. I figured it out one time. The publisher, you know, that I write for, Pampered Music."

"Uh huh, Pampered Music."

"Naturally they like for me to be as productive as possible, but I tell "Em that that's just not the way I operate. I write when I feel like it and when I don't I don't. But I was curious one day and I figured it up and I write on the average of one song a month."

"One a month."

"Yeah, about twelve a year."

"And you record them all yourself?"

"Most of "Em, yeah."

"Well, I know that most of the recordings that we have heard and play over KLEA, are ones you've written and they go over great.

And by the way, many other people record your songs, too."

"I've been fortunate to get some of the real talented people in the business to sing my songs. Of course Patsy Cline had a big song, big record on a thing of mine called, **Crazy**."

"Right."

"And, **Funny How Time Slips Away** *has been a good tune for me, and* **Hello Walls**. *These were songs that were originally recorded by other people.*

"Ah, in the beginning, others recorded 'em before you did?"

"Right."

"How did you get started recording on your own? Were you, ah, say at a recording session where someone else was recording your song or what?"

"Ah, well, I'd been recording for several years before I arrived in Nashville. In fact, a good friend here Tommy Kizziah's with us tonight, and Tommy and I used to work together up around Portland, Oregon, and Vancouver, Washington. And I went down one day in Portland and recorded a thing, and that was the first record I put out was in Portland, and this was in about nineteen fifty-five or six, I believe.

"Can you recall the song now?"

*"Ah, yeah, it was a thing written by Leon Payne, **Lumber Jack**, and the other side was **No Place To Go**, one of my songs. And then from there." He cleared his throat. "Excuse me. Then from there I went to, ah, Pappy Daily's record label. D record label, do you remember the D record company?"*

"Yeah, had a big D on it, right?

"Right."

"Right, mm-hum."

*"And then from there I went to Nashville and recorded for Liberty records, then from Liberty I did one session with Monument. The **I Never Cared For You** record was on Monument, then I went to RCA Victor and I've been with them now for almost three years."*

"Well, I'd say now that's a good performer on a good label right there."

"RCA to me is, ah, the Cadillac of the industry. They're, of course, Chet Atkins is one of the greatest A and R men in the business. He's a genus. We all love "Im in Nashville."

"We'll go along with you on that. I don't guess there's any better than Chet Atkins."

"Not to my knowledge."

"Ah, Willie, as we've said, you've written many good

songs. What's been the top one for you?"

"The songs that I've written myself?"

"Yes."

"Ah, I guess the biggest seller has been **Funny How Time Slips Away***. There's been about seventy something recordings of that song to date."*

"Right. I remember Billy Walker has a good recording of that along with your own."

"Billy Walker had a record on it and so did Johnny Tillison and Joe Hinton and, of course, Doris Day and there's several."

"Right, some of the. . ."

"Pop."

"Pop people, right."

"Perry Como did it."

"That really helps a song when it gets up into that category, doesn't it?"

"Yeah, Perry Como had it in his album. His Nashville album they recorded there, and it's been the biggest seller. I guess that next to that would have to be, maybe, Night Life then **Touch Me** *and then from there I don't know."*

"Yeah, well, it...I'm sure you'd lose track of "Em as many as you've written and have out. Ah, there was something else I would like to ask. What is it that you have right now one of your latest ones that seems to be going real well for ya'? One that you'd like to go or think will?"

"Ah, well, my latest record is **One In A Row***. Ah, for a Christmas release they're re-releasin' ah, this thing that I did on RCA Victor,* **Pretty Paper***, remember that one?"*

"Right, right."

"You'll probably be getting a copy of it around the twenty-fifth of November. And it will be released for Christmas and ah, after the first of the year, ah, I have a song called **The Party's Over***, that will be my next record, my next legitimate release after the first of the year."*

"Yeah, okay, well we'll be looking forward to that one. And I believe you mentioned that you have an album out that was recorded from a live performance?"

"We, ah, one of our, ah, places that we work on the circuit through Texas is a large night club in Fort Worth, Texas, called Panther Hall Ballroom."

"Right."

"And we recorded a live album there sometime in July and it's just been released, and it's actually all they did was just turn the tape machines on and record exactly what we do on the stage every night."

"Right."

"And it was just released and, if the folks would like to have copies of it, maybe they can find it in a record store. I hope so anyway."

"Well, we'll take a look, but just in case we can't find it locally, would you see if you can get us a copy of it."

"I have a copy of it tonight, and I'm gonna see that you have a couple with you before you leave."

"All right, Willie. Good Deal, and we'll see if we can't play it on KLEA. Ah, since it looks like about time for you to have to go back to work out here and entertain the folks a little bit more, I know they're looking forward to it. I believe we'd better let you go.

"We certainly want to thank you for taking the time to chat with us tonight. And anytime you're in Lovington just drop into KLEA, and we'll be glad to talk with ya out there and speak a good word for this country and western Music."

"I'll do it Jim and thank you for coming out. It was nice meetin' ya and talkin' with ya. And be sure and tell all your many listeners thanks for all the help that they've given me and I appreciate it. And we'll see you again next trip."

"Mighty good. Thank you, Willie Nelson."

(End of actual interview.)

Jim clicked off the tape machine. "I think that turned out pretty good."

"So do I, Jim. Thanks again for coming out. I'll get those albums to ya. Tommy, you want one?"

"Yeah, I'd like to have one if you don't mind."

"Are you gonna stick around for another set?"

He looked at Sharon and figured she might be getting tired. "Probably one more is all. I've got to get her home."

Sharon rolled her eyes. "Why, Daddy, I want to stay."

"You look like your getting tired."

"Well, I'm not."

"Whatever you say, baby, but Mamma will kill us both if we're out too late."

"I gotta get back out there. What do you want me to do with the amplifier then, Tommy?" Willie turned to go out of the room.

"Just leave it here, I'll come after it tomorrow."

"Okay. I'll see you next break, if you're here, and get your record."

On the way home from Glen's, Tommy reflected on the way things used to be and how much different his life was now.

A few years back he wouldn't have thought about leaving the dance early, but now it didn't seem quite as important to him. Was it age or had he just lost interest? No, he was still interested or he wouldn't sit in that back room so much playing and singing.

He still loved it, but he guessed his priorities had changed. He glanced over at his little girl. "Did you have fun?"

"Yeah, that was cool. Willie Nelson's nice."

"He's a pretty good ole boy."

"He asked me if I sang."

"What did you tell him?"

"I told him a little. But I think I want to sing more. Maybe even play the guitar or something."

"Now you've had piano lessons, fiddle lessons and took clarinet in school and didn't like any of them. What makes you think you'd like to play guitar?"

"I don't know, I just think it would be fun, that's all. Going with you and Mamma to the dances when I was little was fun, but I was too small to really know what was going on. Tonight, watching Willie Nelson kind of made me want to try it."

He wondered if she really would like guitar. Wouldn't it be great if she started playing and singing? He refused to get his hopes up, but would definitely go and look for her an inexpensive guitar. "Well, we'll see."

It would be great if she could learn a song or two and start singing with his band. He would love to have her along and it would give her some experience. However, he'd only heard her sing a couple of times. It was good but not great. He'd have to see if she could truthfully hold a tune.

Tommy's heart skipped a beat when he saw the twinkle in Sharon's eyes when he gave her the guitar.

"What kind is it, Daddy? I've never seen one like it."

"It's called a Dobro."

"I love it. It's all black and shinny. And what's this big silver thing in the middle?"

"That's what makes it a Dobro, baby. It's a resonator cone. Kind of like a built-in speaker. It gives the guitar a certain tone. They used to always be in acoustic guitars, but this one's electric so you can use it either way."

She rubbed the surface of the guitar. "This is too cool!"

Her reaction was all he needed to justify the cost of the instrument. "I'm glad you like it. Have you picked a song out to learn?"

"Yeah," She sat on the couch and got a piece of paper off the coffee table. "It's called Sad Movies. I wrote the words down earlier."

"Okay, lets go to the back room and listen to the record so I can get the chords for you."

It didn't take him long to figure out the chord progression on the song. Thankfully, there were only three, and it would be an easy song for her to learn to play.

He was surprised at how fast she learned the finger positions on the guitar strings. If she worked at it she would be playing in no time. "It's up to you now. We've gone through the song a couple of times, and you have to do it from here."

"I'll do it, Daddy, you'll see. I won't quit on this, I promise."

"That's good to hear. I have to go back to the school for a little while. Do you want to go?"

"No, I'm going to stay here and practice. I want to sing this for Mamma when she gets home tonight."

Frankie was working the swing shift at the hospital and wouldn't get off until eleven o'clock that night. "Don't forget this is a school night."

"I won't."

The determination he saw on her face was something he hadn't seen when she started learning the other instruments. Maybe this was the one. He walked out of the room and stood for a moment to listen. The chords came slow and the singing was sporadic, but in his heart he knew she was someday going to be a good singer.

Maybe, just maybe, she'd follow in his footsteps. All he could do now was help her when she needed it and sit back and wait.

Frankie walked into the dimly lit living room. Sharon was asleep on the couch. What in the world was that? She walked over to the chair and looked closer. A guitar, a new guitar. Surely Tommy didn't spend money on another guitar he didn't need.

He traded guitars almost like he traded cars. That was one of his favorite pastimes and most of the time it cost them money they didn't have.

Sharon turned over. "Mamma, is that you?"

"Yes, Baby Girl. Why are you still up?"

"I have something to show you." She got up and went over to the guitar. "See what Daddy got me?"

"He got it for you?" Her daughter's smile went from ear to ear and it was hard for her to stay angry with Tommy. She knew what a pushover he was when it came to Sharon and he wanted her to be a singer so bad. She turned the overhead light on.

"It's beautiful, honey, are you going to learn to play it or is it going to be like the rest of the instruments you've wanted to get?"

Sharon took the guitar and sat on the couch. "You'll see."

She strummed a chord. A beautiful, almost grown up voice rang through the house.

"Sad movies always make me cry...sad movies always make me cry... He said he had to work, so I went to the show alone..."

She couldn't believe her ears. Sharon could sing and play the guitar. How wonderful! She knew as proud as she was at this moment that Tommy must have been more proud ten fold. Tears welled in her eyes. Her baby girl was growing up.

Summer 1967

Tommy glanced around the classroom at all the people that were going to graduate tonight. Most of them were younger than him or Mexican.

Was fifty-one years old too old to learn how to read and write? He didn't know and didn't care. He had done it, just like all of the other folks.

He hated having to drive to Hobbs every evening to go to class, but that was part of it. He wanted to read and write. He had to put up with the things he didn't like.

One of those things was reading children's books. He felt silly reading out loud, and writing his ABC'S like a first grader, but that's just what he'd been, a first grader.

Even though he could read and write a little when he began, they made him start at the lowest level. That's the way it should've been if he was going to do it right.

Sharon nudged him from the chair beside his desk. "Daddy, you're not paying attention. They're going to give out the graduation certificates.

She was right. "Sorry."

If it weren't for Sharon, he wouldn't know as much as he did about the class. Never having gone to school, he didn't know how to study. Every night she'd help him with his letters and words.

School wasn't her favorite thing, and she didn't do that well in it, but she could if she applied herself. Frankie told him it said that on almost all of her report cards. Now, he could read her report cards himself.

You wouldn't have known she didn't apply herself. She may not have been a good student, but she was a great teacher.

He supposed she got her helpfulness of other people from her mother. That was a good thing. And he was proud of her leadership.

It had been embarrassing to have his thirteen-year-old daughter help him read a book that said, "Jack and Jill went up the hill," but his payoff came tonight.

"Everyone give a big round of applause to Mr. Kizziah. He has earned his reading and writing certificate and is graduating from class. Mr. Kizziah, would you come up here please and get your certificate?"

The twenty some people in the classroom clapped as he walked up to the young teacher and accepted the piece of paper. If the document didn't mean a thing to anyone else, it meant something to him, the sense of accomplishment.

Chapter 17

July 1970

"Happy birthday to you...Happy birthday to you...Happy birthday dear Sharon...Happy birthday to you."

Tommy watched as everyone gathered around his little girl. She wasn't so little anymore. She'd grown into a beautiful young woman and wanted to come to Oregon for her sixteenth birthday.

It was the first time he'd been back since they moved in sixty-four. The Kizziahs had a couple of family reunions in Texas, so he'd gotten to see some of them there. Myrtle and his brother and sisters had been at the reunions, too. However, Myrt died the year before so he'd never get to see her again. She was the closest thing he had to a mother for most of his life. He was going to miss her.

He studied all the people who were there for the birthday party, and knew they all loved Sharon very much. They were a big part of her life for the first nine years.

Granny Sours was in a wheel chair now, but her spirit was still the same, and she loved giving him grief. She still harped on how much better of a pinochle player she was than him. To tell the truth, she was, but he'd never admit it to her. Why ruin her fun.

Don and Mable Quinn and their son, Chucky, were there, too. Chuck had his seventeenth birthday a couple of months earlier and already had his driver's license. He and Sharon had traipsed all over town, and she loved every minute of it.

She was growing up so fast and his heart was breaking at the thought of her leaving home, getting married and having babies. He was pleased, however, that she'd stuck with playing the guitar. She played good enough to accompany herself and had even written a couple of songs.

Buddy Simmons liked her voice and said she should do some recording. They both knew people in Nashville. That's probably where he should take her. That Tanya Tucker girl had a hit record named Delta Dawn. Sharon learned it as soon as it came out. She could really sing it.

"What are you thinking about, Daddy?"

Her smile went from ear to ear. He kissed her on the cheek. "How lucky I am to have you and Mamma."

She chuckled. "I can't believe everyone is here. Uncle Red, Aunt Dee, Janie, Aunt Jessie and Uncle Jack, Darlene, Arlene, Trina, Margaret, and everyone else. This is the best birthday I've ever had. And Chucky's so cute."

Why did he know that was coming? "I'm glad we could give you what you wanted for your birthday."

"Me, too. Thanks, Daddy."

"You're welcome, Baby." He watched her walk away.

Her pretty pink dress clung to her tall thin frame. She was going to be a full-grown woman soon and the signs of her hourglass figure were already evident.

He put his arm around his wife's waist. "Mamma, I'm going to have to get my shotgun out soon."

She furrowed her brow and met his gaze. "What for?"

Smiling he replied. "To keep the boys away from our baby."

Her gaze followed his to where Sharon stood with Chucky beside Granny Sours. "Yes, I think you are."

Fall 1971

Tommy's heart went out to his good friend, Buddy

Simmons, as he listened to the concerned man's voice from the other end of the telephone.

"Tommy, it was the same motor cycle he had last year when y'all were out here. The one Sharon was riding through the back lot at the house. Remember when it fell on her and she got that big burn on her calf?"

"I remember. It scared the hell out of us."

"Well, that's just about the same place they had to amputate Don's leg from. It's gone from the knee down. You can imagine what we've been going through."

He heard a cry in Buddy's voice and knew the poor man had tears in his eyes.

"He's so young. He has the rest of his life in front of him and now this. Damn it all!"

"Buddy, my heart's with you, my friend. I wish there was something I could do." This man had been his confidant for many years and now he wasn't there when he needed him.

Buddy sniffed and caught his breath. "Well, Tom, actually there is something you and Frankie can do."

"You name it."

"Don wants to come to your house to recover. He loves you and Frankie and Sharon so much. Sharon makes him laugh and you and Frankie have been like his second parents."

Now that was something they could help with. "We'd love to have him. When will he be here?"

"Don't you need to talk to Frankie first?"

"Hells bells, Buddy, you know she loves your boys. Besides she's a nurse and loves to nurture people, you know that. No, I don't need to talk to her. Send him on."

"Okay, I'll make arrangements with the airline and call you back."

"Now, we don't have an airport here, but there's one in Midland and one in Lubbock. I'll go pick him up at either place. They're both about the same distance from here, so you just pick the cheapest route."

"Thank you, Tom. He's going to be excited. Opal and I are grateful to have friends like you two."

"You're welcome, Buddy. I'll be waiting for your call."

Spring 1972

"Sharon Kizziah!"

Tommy squeezed Frankie's hand when their daughter walked across the stage at Lovington High School and accepted her diploma. "Look at her, Mamma." Her black hair shone in the sunlight. "Isn't she a beauty?"

Frankie nodded her head and wiped a tear from her eye. He was proud of Sharon for graduating. He'd worried about it because she was so disinterested in school. The only thing she liked about it was choir.

The last time he'd seen her on this stage was a year earlier during production called "Up Up and Away." Sharon and her friend had a spot singing. Sharon played the guitar to accompany them and the audience went wild.

Soon he and Frankie would take her to Nashville. He had some connections there and intended to get her into a record company somewhere.

He had so much confidence in her; he knew she could be a star. The only thing that worried him was the fact that she had a boyfriend, and they seemed to be getting serious. He hoped she didn't throw her life away by getting married. She was so young and talented.

Admitting that his marriage to Frankie, no matter how much he loved her, was probably the reason he wasn't a star. He'd felt obligated to keep a steady job to support her and the boys. Then Sharon came along, and he was getting too old to make the proper moves to promote himself.

That's why he made up his mind to do everything in his power to encourage his little girl not to marry, but to go forward in a singing career. They'd be leaving for Tennessee in three weeks.

1970's

TJ, Red, Bill, Mary, Tommy and Jack

Bill and second wife Wilma

Frankie and Red

Jack's wife Jessie and Reuben

Bill, old time medicine show friend Greasy medley, Bill's boy Byron and Tommy

Byron and Mary

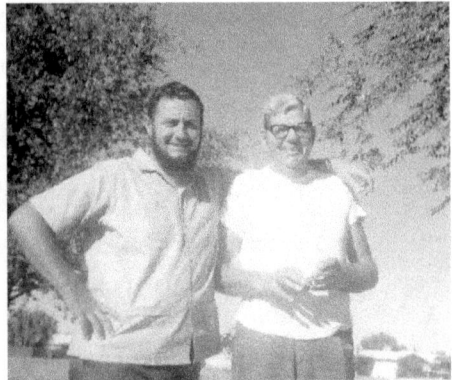

Jack's boy Jackie and Tommy

Christy, Susan and Amy Drum Mary's granddaughter's

Frankie and Tommy

Sharon, Tommy and Mary

Sharon and Tommy

Frankie, Sharon and Tommy 1972

Tommy

Jack's wife Jessie & Reuben

Margie & TJ Kizziah

Margie & Tommy

Mary & Reuben Allen

Mary

Red & Tommy

TJ & Bill

Red, Mary & Frankie

* * *

December 1972

"Are you sure this is what you want, Sharon? It's not too late to back out." Tommy tried to read his daughter's true feelings by looking deep into her big brown eyes.

"Yes, Daddy, it is. Stop worrying."

"That's my job."

"Well, that's why you have stomach trouble. Stop it."

She was so beautiful in her long white wedding dress. He had been heart broken that she didn't put everything she had into the trip to Nashville, but there was nothing he could do about that now. It had been her decision and all he wanted was for her to be happy.

However, he didn't think this was the right guy for her, but again, it was her decision.

He smiled and kissed her on the cheek. "I'll try." He turned and went outside the church to wait for the ceremony to start.

So many things had happened that year. Besides Sharon's graduation, going to Nashville and now her wedding. Isom Collier, Frankie's father, died. He was a great old man and quite well known and loved in town.

He thought his wife was going to lose her mind when they walked by her daddy's casket for the last time. It had been in the very church they were in now.

The poor woman cried out, "Daddy, that's my daddy." She leaned over the casket and held the old man as well as she could. "Daddy, oh, daddy," she sobbed.

It was all he could do to pull her away. He'd never seen her like that before and never wanted to again.

One really good event that year was when his second granddaughter was born. The oldest granddaughter, Shannon was five now and a pretty little thing. She was going to be in the wedding. The baby, Shelly, was only two months old.

Family and friends gathered for Sharon's wedding day. He guessed he'd better get inside so he could do something he didn't really want to do. Give her away.

* * *

Summer 1982
Tommy leaned back on the cold vinyl chair in the hospital room. He didn't like waiting, but the nurse wouldn't let him walk downstairs by himself, she insisted he ride in a wheel chair. It was probably for the best. He didn't know if he'd have the strength to walk that far anyway.

Open-heart surgery was something he never wanted to go through again. Technology had come so far in his sixty-seven years on this earth. He'd watched the world change right before his eyes. Thank God doctors could do the things they did or he probably wouldn't be alive.

The last few years had brought about many changes in life for Frankie and him.

In '73' Ike died. He was the first in his generation to pass. The realization of mortality started setting in way back then.

Sharon divorced her husband in '74'. She'd gotten in a band and gone on the road for a short time, and when she came home, he was having an affair with the next-door neighbor.

Man did he want to hurt that man for doing that to his little girl, but at least she was rid of him and moving forward in her music. He was just thankful she didn't have any babies.

Jack and Red came out from Oregon that year. It was good to see them.

Sharon moved to Lubbock in '75'. She'd been in different bands around and he knew from experience that she wouldn't always be in the music business. If she didn't make it big, he didn't want her to be like him. He wanted her to have a trade to fall back on. He and Frankie talked her into going to barber school. She graduated from there in '76'

It was funny how she followed in his footsteps. His good friend Faron Young was a guest star with one of the bands Sharon was in '76'. She'd made a trip to Lovington a few days after his appearance and wrote a note saying "Tell Dad Faron Young said hi and he loves him." He felt the wallet he carried in his back pocket. That note was still in there and it had been five years. Every now and again a thread of his musical career would cross his path.

Benny and Patsy had tried for years to have a child, finally in '76' they succeeded. He had his first grandson. Daron was a great kid, but they lived in Dallas and he didn't get to see him much.

Johnny and Pat lived in El Reno, Oklahoma. She hoped both boys would move closer to home, but it didn't look like that was going to happen any time soon. Pat had their third daughter in '77'. All of their girls' names started with an s. Shannon, Shelly and Sarah, who came out with red hair. He was sure Den Jones was proud of that. At least one of his grandkids was a redhead.

A lady from Austin, Texas, heard Sharon sing at a nightclub in Lubbock in '78' and decided she wanted to put some money behind her. His heart broke when she took up with a man and blew the deal. She must have loved him, though because she married him and they moved back to Lovington in '79'.

It was good to have her home. She opened a barber shop and put together a band. They played in a lounge in Hobbs and he'd go over and sit in with them often. Even at his age, he still missed the business, but at least he could go where his baby was playing and sing with her group, Hickory Wind.

Mary's husband died in '79'. He was such a good man. Everyone loved Reuben. Mary had been lost at first, but her kids helped her through it and she was bette every day.

He'd quit his job with the school system some years earlier and went to work for the City of Lovington. He had a small group of musicians that played at the Senior Citizens dances with him for the last decade.

Now, it was 1982 and if it hadn't been for his brother Bill a couple of weeks earlier, he wouldn't have known he, too, was about to have a full blown heart attack. The stress of Bill's death brought on the stress that probably caused the chest pains to start.

Red and Jack came for the funeral and were there for his surgery. They waited to see if he was going to live through the ordeal before they headed home. Both of them looked so old. Hells bells, they were old.

The nurse entered the room with the wheelchair. "Mr. Kizziah, your wife is waiting with the car, I guess you're ready to go home."

He took a seat and as the lady pushed him through the hallways of the Methodist hospital in Lubbock, he realized his brothers weren't the only ones aging. For the first time in his life he was aware that he was getting old.

Fall 1983

"Tommy, you're wanted on the phone." Frankie handed him the receiver.

"Who is it?"

"I don't know, he asked for Sonny Rogers."

Sonny Rogers? Who the hell would be calling him that? "Hello."

"Mr. Rogers?"

"Well, it depends on who's calling."

"I'm Glenn Hinson. Mr. Rogers, I'm putting together an old time medicine show in New York City. I want to bring back some of the folks that were on the original shows years ago. Everyone who I've contacted has told me I need to get hold of Sonny Rogers. It took me awhile to find you, if, in fact, I have the right person. If I do, I'd like to talk to you about being on the show."

A medicine show in New York? Hells bells, this sounded interesting. "In that case, yes, this is Sonny Rogers. I haven't gone by that name since I was a young man, so you can call me Tommy, Tommy Kizziah."

"Yes, Mr. Kizziah, it took me forever to find out your real name. Everyone knew you as Sonny."

"Well, tell me what this is all about."

"I'm going to produce an old time medicine show at the well known off Broadway theater, The American Place. I already have a few old-timers to be on the show, and some of them recommended that I get in touch with you. Do you still sing, Mr. Kizziah?"

"I do a little pickin' and grinnin' now and then."

"Well, I'd like to come to your home and visit with you to see if you would be right for the show."

"That sounds good, but I can't afford a trip to New York City."

"Mr. Kizziah, if you're on the show, it's all expenses paid. You won't have to put out a dime. Plus, we'll give you a pay check at the end of the two week run."

"Hold on a minute."

"Okay."

He put his hand over the mouthpiece of the phone. "Mamma, this is a man from New York. They might want me to be in a show there. He wants to come visit us. It won't cost anything for me to go and they are going to pay me."

"That sounds wonderful. Don't keep him waiting, tell him to come on."

"Mr. Hinson, I'm very interested. When could you be here?"

"Is next week too soon?"

"That's fine. I'll see you soon."

He never had liked airplanes and he didn't like them any better now. He was glad to be on the ground in New York City and was excited to start rehearsals.

The back seat of the limousine was plush. There were going to be a lot of first time things on this trip, he could tell. It was strange to be separated from the driver, but at least the man knew where he was going. If he had to drive, he'd be totally lost.

Buildings towered over the vehicle on all sides. People hustled and bustled along the sidewalks. He'd never seen so many people walking before. Where were they all going? Hells bells, this was sure a different world than Lovington, New Mexico.

The window between him and the driver went down. "This is it, Mr. Kizziah," the man said, pulling into the circle drive of a huge motel. "You'll be staying here for the next few weeks, hope you enjoy it."

"Oh, I will, I'm sure."

The driver carried his bags and led the way inside and to the front desk. "This is Tommy Kizziah. He's with the American Place show and has reservations."

"Yes, they are all in the same wing."

Tommy was amazed. He didn't have to do a thing but get settled into his room. He'd met with all the other folks who were on the show and had known only a couple of them.

At his age, this would probably be the last big show of his life. He only wished some of his family members could be here to see it. By himself or not, he was going to enjoy every minute of his stay.

* * *

It was the last night of The Vitonka Medicine Show at The American Place Theater. Tommy couldn't believe the time had gone by so fast, but tomorrow he'd be leaving this great city to go home.

Inside his small dressing room, he tightened his necktie and studied the reflection of the old man in the mirror. His hair was solid white, but he was thankful God had seen to it he hadn't lost any of it. The bright hazel eyes that should have been looking back at him were now a bit faded. Funny, he didn't feel any different inside, but he damn sure looked different on the outside.

This experience had been one of the best ones of his life. Why, the president of the stock exchange had come to see the show one night and liked his performance so well the next day the man sent a limo to pick him up and take him to the Exchange. There was nothing to compare to what he saw that day from the upper level of the room. Those people were crazy. How they understood the signals and shouts he'd never know, but somehow they got the job done.

CNN interviewed him for the T.V. news. He called home and told Frankie. She said everyone in Lovington saw it. On the national news at the age of sixty-eight! What a deal.

His wildest dreams wouldn't have put him here at this time in his life. It was great to play in front of a large audience again. His heart felt heavy in his chest, knowing it would be over after one more presentation.

He glanced at his watch. Time to go. His turn would be coming up soon.

(Tommy's actual part in the Vitonka Medicine Show.)
"Right now it's time for a singer of sweet ballads. Here is Tommy Kizziah."

Applause rang through the theater when he made his entrance. Only one stool and two microphones occupied the center of the stage floor and the spotlight was on him.

He took a seat on the stool and adjusted the vocal mic. so it was perfectly placed. "Thank ya, sir, and I'd like to say howdy to ya, friends, and welcome to our program. We hope that you're gettin' your enjoys out of it.

"This particular song was written about an old blind fiddler and that's the title of it. It's a true story."

His heart was beating hard in his chest. No matter how many times he did this, he was always nervous. He put his acoustic guitar on his knee. A lone fiddle player stood in the shadows.

He strummed his guitar, took a deep breath and started to sing; **"When I was just a kid I'd go to town on Saturday. On the street I'd listen to the old blind fiddler play. He was close to no one his life was almost gone, but to me he was my friend and always played such pretty songs..."**

He loved to hear the hand clapping and whistles from the audience. It was time for his next song.

"A pop song in the twenties, thirties, forties, I'm sure a lot of you remember it. A little step-it-up-and-go type thing."

"Please don't talk about me when I'm gone." The crowd's reaction told him they did remember the tune. **"Though our friendship ceases from now on. If you can't say anything that's nice..."**

The air crackled with applause and he wished the night would never end. He'd like nothing more than to sit here and sing for these people.

"I wish, since you liked that one so well, I could do all of them in that particular style for ya. But my daughter says, now Daddy if you go up there and don't sing my song, I might not speak to you for...thirty seconds." He knew that would get a chuckle out of them.

"And this is one that I don't like to sing, but I will, and the reason I don't like to is...well, after I get into it, you'll know the reason why."

"In a vine covered shack in the mountain. Bravely fighting the battle of time. Lives a dear one who's weathered life's sorrows. It's that silver haired daddy of mine.

If I could recall all the heartaches Dear Old Daddy I've caused you to bear. If I could erase those lines from your face and bring back the gold to your hair. If God would but grant me the power, just to turn back the pages of time. I

would give all I own if I could put a tone to that silver haired daddy of mine.

Though I know it's too late, Dear Old Daddy, to repay all the sorrows and cares, though dear mother she's waiting up in heaven, just to comfort and solace you there.

Now if I could recall the heartaches, Dear Old Daddy, I've caused you to bear. If I could erase those lines from your face and bring back the gold to your hair. Now, if God would but grant me the power, just to turn back the pages of time. I would give all I own if I could put a tone to that silver haired daddy of mine.

(End of Tommy's part in show.)

He strummed the last note on the guitar and let it ring. Some of the folks in the New York audience were weeping. Their appreciation of what he'd done for them that evening was evident when they stood in honor of his talent.

It was over. Tears rolled down his cheek as he said a silent prayer to thank God for allowing him this very special opportunity. He took his last bow

1980's

Buddy & Opal Simmons

Evelyn, Buddy and Evelyn's
husband Al

Don & Larry Simmons

Jack in character as
Dorothy

Jack & Sharon

Jackie, Jessie, Jack, Janie, Jody & John Thomas

Jack & Jessie

Jack

Red & Jack

Red, Mary, Bill, Tommy & Jack

Tommy & Frankie

Frankie, Sharon &
Tommy

Tommy performing with
Hickory Wind
Dennis & Sharon's band

Sharon & Frankie

YOUNG TOM KIZZIAH

Tom Kizziah has been in the music business since he was seven years old. He is pictured with his guitar and one of his many recordings. Born in Rockwood, Tennessee, Kizziah has played from coast to coast. He and his wife, Frankie, met in Lubbock, Texas, at the old Lubbock Hotel where he was playing. They were married in Oregon.

MEDICINE SHOW MAN

Tom Kizziah was producer and leading man in a medicine show for approximately 10 years during the years when the shows were such popular entertainment. Kizziah underwent heart surgery and says he is completely recovered. He began singing three weeks after surgery to expand his lungs. He is excited about the medicine show in which he will participate that will open the 20th anniversary season at the American Place, located one block from Broadway in New York City. The cast will be entirely from medicine show veterans, including Tom Kizziah of Lovington.

Article in The Lovington Leader before Tommy went to N.Y. to do the Vi-Ton-Ka Medicine Show

Tommy backstage at the American Place Theater getting ready to perform

SHOWBILL®

AMERICAN PLACE THEATRE

THE VI-TON-KA MEDICINE SHOW

THE AMERICAN PLACE THEATRE

Director
WYNN HANDMAN

Associate Director
JULIA MILES

presents

THE VI-TON-KA MEDICINE SHOW

An Authentic Recreation of an American Theatrical Tradition

with

FRED F. BLOODGOOD
JAMES "GOOBER" BUCHANAN
COL. BUSTER DOSS
ERNEST W. HAYES
DEWITT "SNUFFY" JENKINS
TOMMY KIZZIAH
HAROLD LUCAS
RANDY LUCAS
DALE MADDEN, SR.
DALE "BOOTS" MADDEN
MARY SMITH McCLAIN
CONNIE MILLS
HOMER "PAPPY" SHERRILL
LEROY WATTS

Project Director
GLENN HINSON

Associate Project Director
C. LEE JENNER

Staging & Design Consultant
BROOKS McNAMARA

Sets and Lights by
MARCO A. MARTINEZ-GALARCE

Production Supervisor
NANCY HARRINGTON

OCTOBER 1983

Johnny   Frankie   Tommy   Sharon   Benny
Tommy with his family, after the memorial service of his mother-in-law, Lena Collier. This was six days before his death

EPILOGUE

Tommy Kizziah left New York after the Vitonka Medicine show and went back to Lovington, New Mexico where he lived out the remainder of his life.

In nineteen eighty-six Tommy was diagnosed with carotid artery stenosis. Surgery was done to remove fat and plaque from the artery on the left side of his neck.

During this kind of surgery, doctors insert a balloon type device into the throat to cut off the blood circulation of the artery. In Tommy's case when the device was inserted, it was placed inside the vocal chords. This caused the chord on the left side to become paralyzed. He was devastated.

Each day he practiced, and though his voice did improve some over time, he could never sing again.

He died of a massive heart attack December sixteenth, nineteen eighty-nine.

Spring 2005

Tommy's brother T.J., making his home in Mississippi (soon to move to Texas) with his second wife Margie, is the only living child left that was born to Rebeka and Lon Kizziah. T.J. never had children, but loves and enjoys his stepchildren and grandchildren.

Born to Myrtle and Lon Kizziah were Ivy, Ella Maud and Jimmy. Unfortunately, Jimmy passed in 2003 from diabetes complications, but Ivy and Ella still live in Brenham, Texas.

Ivy married Wesley Kettler and they had one son, Randy. Randy was diagnosed with terminal cancer in 2003 and died in February, 2004.

Ella and her first husband had a son they named Rory. Rory was killed in a car accident at the young age of eighteen. Ella divorced and is now remarried to a wonderful man named Reinhardt.

Jack Kizziah died in nineteen eighty-four, Mary in nineteen eighty-seven and Red passed in nineteen eighty-nine.

Jack and Red's wives have both passed, but their children are doing well. All of them, but Jack Jr., live in Salem, Oregon. Jack Jr. is in Washington state.

The members of the West Coast Ramblers remained friends over all the years. Johnny Reese, Ed Zunck and Ed Whittaker are all deceased.

Buddy Simmons is in Portland, Oregon, with his wife Opal. Their sons Don and Larry perform on the west coast with their bands. Don's son, Dean Simmons, is a well-known Garth Brooks imitator in Las Vegas and around the country.

Evelyn, a survivor of breast cancer, lives with her husband, Al, in Salem, Oregon.

Ray (Skipper) Montee is in Portland with his wife, Sally. He is still involved in music, though he doesn't play his steel guitar as much as he used to. He says the West Coast Ramblers were the best band he ever played with.

Tommy's stepson, Benny Jones, is a retired high school baseball coach. He and his wife Patsy live on a lake not far from Dallas. Their son, Daron, lives and works in Dallas and is not married.

Johnny and his wife Pat are only thirty miles from Frankie, in Denver City, Texas. Shannon, their oldest daughter has two girls and lives in Austin, Texas. Shelly, the middle girl had two daughters and resides in Lovington. Sarah, the youngest, is due to graduate from college in May 2004.

Sharon met and married her third husband, Dennis. Both being musicians, they spent many years on the road playing to their fans. She never had children, but like her father, loves her stepchildren and grandchildren. She and Dennis now live in Springfield, Missouri where they are both barbers and own their own shop. They still play publicly now and then.

The note she wrote to her dad in nineteen-seventy-six telling him Faron Young loved him, is now in her wallet. Her father carried it in his until the day he died.

Frankie Kizziah is alive and well at eighty one years of age. She resides in Lovington, New Mexico. Since the death of her husband, she has remained close to the Simmons family and the wives of deceased members of the Ramblers.

She lives for her children and grandchildren and is very close to all of them. She still loves and misses her beloved husband immensely. He and his friends and family are reunited and playing their music for all of heaven. Even though he didn't become a well-known artist in the music business, he will always be a shining star in her heart.

2000's

TJ Kizziah ~ Aberdeen, MS

Martha Monroe, Ella Kramer & Ivy Kettler ~ Brenham, TX
Jimmie Rogers Kizziah died in 2003

Frankie & Johnny

Frankie & Benny

Johnny's wife Pat

Benny's wife Patsy

Sharon & Dennis

Johnny & Benny

Frankie & Sharon

Benny & Patsy's
son Daron

Johnny & Pat's daughters
Sarah, Shelly & Shannon

Sharon was born in 1954. Her dad was a musician and her mom a nurse. She inherited her father's musical talents, and at the age of 12 began writing songs. At 19 she went on the road with a band of her won.

Knowing she wouldn't be playing music all of her life, her parents suggested she go to barber school. She interrupted her music career and attended barber collage, in Lubbock Texas.After graduation, she went right back to playing music.

In 1979 she met guitar player, Dennis Holmes. For the next few years their band, Hickory Wind, played music in Canada, Alaska and 20 of the lower 48 states. Dennis and Sharon married in 1990.

They moved to the Ozarks and Sharon cut hair and played music until she retired from the music business in 1996. She became interest in writing romance novels. Her first book, Ride the Storm, was published in May of 2002.

She and her husband, who attended barber school in 1996. now own A Barber Shop in the Ozarks and have recently opened a professional recording studio. Sharon spends her spare time writing playing in the studio and enjoying her family and her dogs.